The symbolism of style

Rita Simon, a founder member of the art therapy profession, has for over forty years been developing her understanding of the complex interplay between content and style in patients' work. In *The Symbolism of Style* she argues that, while a picture can speak through both its content and its style, it is the *style* that reflects the patient's unconscious attitude to life.

Rita Simon looks at the progression of style in children's work and traces the developmental stages to which it is sometimes helpful for an adult to return, albeit temporarily. She shows that in the early stages of therapy, the style can help the art therapist to understand a patient's underlying mood; and later, a change in style can indicate a radical change in a patient's grasp of reality. Rita Simon believes that the therapist's understanding of the hidden meaning in the style can greatly enrich the therapeutic process and improve its outcome. The patient can be understood on a deep level without verbal interventions that inevitably interrupt the integrative drive of the visual symbolism. From her years of study of clinical material, she has developed a classification of the four basic styles that recur in patients' work. She devotes a chapter to each style, illustrating its significance with copious case material from the work of both adults and children.

Lavishly illustrated in colour and black-and-white, *The Symbolism of Style* is an important contribution to the exploration of the content and symbolism of imagery, placing the image firmly in the centre of art therapy practice.

Rita Simon has worked for many years as an art therapist both in private practice and in the NHS. She frequently lectures and holds workshops in London, Ireland and Scandinavia.

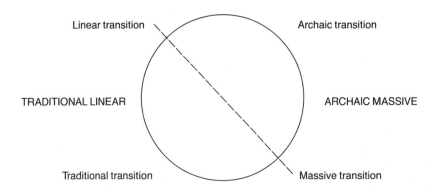

Figure 1.1 The circle of styles

Four basic styles of art are recognized: they are located at four points of the compass and are indicated in the diagram by capital letters. These styles are linked by transitional areas in which there is generally an overlap of the character-istic features of the adjacent areas. This overlap in the properties of the adjacent areas creates four transitional styles making eight styles in all.

Some art works use only one style: others contain more than one. Movement from one style to another is generally in a clockwise direction, although during therapy there may be some anticlockwise movement.

Two basic styles are Archaic and two are Traditional. The division lies diagon-ally in the position indicated by a dotted line.

Children's art usually starts at the Archaic Linear position and develops clock-wise round the circle. In Western cultural tradition continuity is broken during latency when further change would overlap the original Archaic Linear style.

The symbolism of style

Art as therapy

R.M. Simon

Tavistock/Routledge
London and New York

First published in 1992
by Routledge
11 New Fetter Lane, London EC4P 4EE

Simultaneously published in the USA and Canada
by Routledge
a division of Routledge, Chapman and Hall Inc.
29 West 35th Street, New York, NY 10001

Typeset in 10/12 Times by
Leaper & Gard Limited, Bristol
Printed and bound in Great Britain by Biddles Ltd,
Guildford and King's Lynn

British Library Cataloguing in Publication Data
Simon, Rita, *1921*–
   The symbolism of style.
   I. Title
   615.85156

Library of Congress Cataloging in Publication Data
also available

ISBN 0–415–04130–9
     0–415–04131–7 (pbk)

... A symbol is NOT a sign for something that can just as well be expressed in rational words, that is why Freud really uses the term 'symbol' incorrectly. A stick for instance is not a symbol for a sex organ but merely a sign or 'cipher'; his 'symbol' does not in any way express more than can also be expressed in another or a rational way. ... Where a symbol is needed as expression of experience every other mode of expression would be inadequate.

Once they (the symbols) are fully analysed and formulated they lose their original significance as symbols.

(Adler 1948: 49)

To my husband, for his help and encouragement

Contents

List of illustrations

Preface

This book is intended for those therapists who encourage their patients to use art materials without thought or direction. Much of it preaches to the converted but some of it is new.

I believe that when creative art is offered as a means of helping disturbed adults and children it should be held distinct from verbal psychotherapy. These two aspects of help are not mutually exclusive, for most of us talk with our patients and also sit quietly and support what they do by our concerned attention. However, because we rely on words as the clearest means of understanding, it is very easy for both patient and therapist to overlook the realization that has arisen without words, within the art work itself. I am convinced that all creative art practice has an integrating effect upon the artist and promotes mental health. My ideas about the way this happens have developed very slowly over nearly fifty years of work with disturbed adults and children, and I hope that they may have some general use for other therapists. I have done very little to look for a general application of my ideas apart from two papers (1976, 1984). Obviously, research is still needed if any general principles are to be established.

Writing about non-verbal experience is a painful work of translation. The faithfulness of such a translation can only be accepted when it enlightens similar experiences for the reader. By making an artificial division between style and content I can focus attention upon style and describe the meaning it offers; for the same reason I have discussed reverie as if it were apart from fantasy, although I have no evidence that it is a separate mental state. My temperament, my training, and my work with patients makes me rather independent of words. Visual images often seem the most direct and economic means of realization: it is quite a different matter when it is necessary to describe these realizations in cold prose. I am aware how often I fail to convey the poetry of creative expression, the dance of liberated movement when a brushful of colour swings across the paper and the patient frees himself from his sense of helplessness. The publisher's generosity in allowing me to use so many illustrations has greatly helped to make up for my verbal deficiencies.

I begin the work with a sort of autobiographical sketch, showing the way in which my ideas developed and the major influences that contributed to them. Chapter 1 offers the theoretical viewpoint and Chapter 2 gives an example of its use in a brief therapeutic intervention. Chapter 3 focuses upon the developmental styles of children as they reflect the whole system of art styles. The rest of the book considers each style in a chapter of its own, allowing for the inevitable overlaps that occur when case studies are offered as examples.

Throughout the book patients are referred to as masculine simply to avoid clumsy constructions.

I would like to show my gratitude to the many people who have encouraged me over the years in this work. I hope that all know, or have known, how much I appreciate their support. First, my thanks go to those who introduced me to the idea that art was therapy, and then to those who have helped me write about it.

It was Dr Joshua Bierer who first asked me to work with patients, and Dr Eric Strauss who found me a personal analyst in Dr Lovel Barnes. I was greatly stimulated by discussions with Professor Ralph Pickford, Dr Joyce Martin, Dr Alice Buck, Dr Charlie Robinson, Dr Gordon Cross and Dr Peter Wells. Irene Champernoune, Adrian Hill and Margaret Lyddiatt were good friends. Sister Leonie Bowland generously lent me her fine collection of children's drawings and Dr Ronald Hamilton supported my work with geriatric patients. My son David continually stimulates my ideas from the perspective of family therapy and Elinor Ulman's editorial work on many of my papers helped me to become more precise in my writing. I am particularly indebted to Marion Milner on two counts. Her book *On Not Being Able To Paint* came out in 1950 at the time of my early struggles to understand patients' art, and her brilliant insights into the psychoanalytic meaning of doodles encouraged me to look deeper. I am also indebted to her for reading this book in manuscript and making many helpful suggestions. Most of all I am indebted to all those adults and children who, when patients, shared themselves with me during the therapeutic sessions.

Being an artist by temperament and training, words have not written themselves for me in this book; however, if I had not been a practising artist I would have been less aware of style as distinct from content in art. My main difficulty has been in creating a theoretical structure to explain how I understand what happens when art is therapy, since the practice came from intuitive responses so many years before a rationalizing theory could be attempted. I feel that this is the way it should be – because it is the only way round for me. Although my approach is empirical it is not entirely objective, for my task is not only to observe; sometimes I am needed to respond, to reply, or to participate. These interventions naturally change the quality of my observation. I have described my work as truly and precisely as I can but

We all write legends – who has not observed in himself, in his ordinary dealings with the facts of everyday life, with the sayings and doings of his acquaintances – in short with everything that comes before him as a FACT – a disposition to forget the real order in which they appear and arrange them according to his theory of how they ought to be.

(Froude 1900)

Introduction
The hidden meaning of style in art therapy

More than forty years ago I was asked if I would volunteer to teach some psychiatric patients to paint. My reluctant acceptance then has since led to a most rewarding way of life. At that time artists were not generally considered to be proper people to work with the insane – perhaps they seemed to be too near the edge themselves, and living a bohemian or immoral way of life. Artists who were mad, or became mad, gave colour to the notion that madness was akin to genius.

I was hardly more than a student, having first studied fine art for six years and then specialized in book production, and was working for a publisher in war-time London. I was attending life classes for some evenings a week and when I set up a weekly group for patients in my home I was immediately impressed by their commitment to drawing and painting, by comparison with the often jaded atmosphere in a conventional art class. Although I was prepared to lend studio space to the patients, I was not at all interested in teaching them and was relieved to find that they were not interested in being taught. When I offered the simplest materials such as powder paint, pastels, charcoal and clay they seized on them and were completely absorbed in original, creative work. They did not consider the completed work as art; they were quite happy to work on the backs of old posters, as we could not afford cartridge paper: charcoal or pastel drawings became smudged and the clay was put back in the bin after use. It was my own interest, rather than theirs, that led me to keep the pictures in newspaper folders, initialled and dated. Occasionally a patient would look back over his work and make a surprising comment about it, recalling his state of mind, that I had not known at the time. I had no idea why these people were so eager to come but I was aware that something important was going on. Although they did not show any interest in the works of art in museums and art galleries it was obvious that they needed to express themselves through art.

The paintings did not look amateur: they did not imitate art, and were more like the works of original artists or children in their directness. Their intensity was startling. I wanted very much to know what was going on but

knew no one to ask and was averse to reading psychology or psychotherapy, clinging to the feeling that only the actual experience of seeing the
art work and watching the way it came about could properly teach me. I am
still not happy to go far from the work process in the search for the
meaning of art as a therapy. I feel that I understand best when I watch an
image unfold in all its unexpectedness – showing the life of the inner person
I do not meet in any other way.

Since those days I have read a great deal about psychotherapy and
psychoanalysis as well as what has been written about art therapy.
Although much of Freud's theory has been invaluable for my own slow-
developing view it will become obvious that I am not a 'Freudian'. I am not
a 'Jungian' either, although I am indebted to aspects of Jung's work,
particularly his study of psychological types (Jung 1963) which has helped
me to see beyond my own art style and its preferences and prejudices.

In 1950 I came across the book *On Not Being Able To Paint* by Marion
Milner (under the pseudonym of Joanna Field), whose self-revelation was
tremendously helpful to me. In 1983 I eventually met Marion Milner and
shared some of my enthusiasm with her. I did not know about the work of
Donald Winnicott until I bought his book *Playing and Reality* in 1971;
these works have been a continual source of enrichment for me. Although I
had been drawn into art therapy by an Adlerian and still greatly value the
mental freedom he instilled in his staff at the day hospital and his provision
of a setting for the art group, I cannot claim to be an Adlerian. In making
these confessions I realize that I may alienate some of those whom I would
like to address, but the fact remains that I cherished ignorance then, and
even now still value the creative potential that can accompany it, for
without ignorance there can be no originality, even if one's discoveries are
of things already well known to others.

When the Alderian analyst, Joshua Bierer, set up the first psychiatric day
hospital in 1944 I was offered a part-time appointment there with a room
and equipment for the art sessions. I had opportunities to meet the doctors
at weekly case meetings and also other psychiatrists who were interested in
the day hospital movement and psychiatric social clubs. At a meeting
convened by the National Association for Mental Health in the late 1940s,
I met Adrian Hill, an art teacher who, although himself partly disabled by
the effects of pulmonary tubercolosis, pioneered the idea of art activities for
physically ill and 'shell-shocked' patients, both here and in Canada and
South Africa. His approach widened my idea of the therapeutic value of art
in cases where normally healthy people were mentally upset by a physical
condition that interfered with their previously satisfactory way of life.
Through such contacts I began to give individual sessions to many different
types of patient in general hospitals and sanatoria. I was invited to set up an
art group for long-stay schizophrenic patients, and later this group was able
to stay on in the art room and make tea; they then agreed to invite a

psychiatrist to look at their paintings with them. In those days, before the sophistication of chemotherapy, it seemed rather miraculous that patients who had been institutionalized for up to fourteen years, and were normally quite withdrawn, could make such a social commitment. The notes I took of these sessions were a valuable contribution to my understanding of what was going on.

I came to find this work with patients far more interesting than my professional life as a commercial artist, but before moving wholly into the area of therapy I felt I needed to look further at the differences between the art student and the art patient. This led me to part-time art school teaching for two years. I could see that patients who were desperately ill, or traumatized following an accident, used the art materials in the same sort of way as psychiatric patients and children. However, those who were less stressed or recovering had greater difficulty in working. They seemed more amateur, and very few continued to draw or paint once they were back to normal life. I also met a third type of patient who was eager to work at first but soon preferred to spend the time talking to me, as I seemed a sympathetic listener. Although it was flattering to be taken into their confidence I felt inadequate and afraid of failing their expectations by seeming to offer psychological skills I had not got. When I transferred the original group from my home to the day hospital they saw me as a member of the therapeutic team rather than as an artist offering them the use of a studio. At first I tried to be helpful by looking at the ideas behind the subject of a patient's work in terms of Freudian or Jungian symbolism, but I put these theories aside as I soon found myself out of my depth. As will be seen, years later some of these ideas fell into place but at that time I did not have the experience to cope with them and I had to accept that the type of patient who needed 'therapeutic talk' would give up art work if he could not find satisfaction in the use of non-verbal expression alone. As a result of my own analysis I came to understand their attitude better; then I found that many of these difficulties could be avoided. At the time I could only fall back on some simple suggestions when patients could not continue painting, such as returning to a previous painting and extending it in some way, or mounting it on a large piece of paper so that it could expand in any direction. My suggestions were made timidly, for I was afraid to interfere; as an art student I had cut classes often enough in order to avoid an over-enthusiastic teacher.

I began to ask the advice of doctors and art teachers and had the good fortune to meet the Jungian analyst and psychiatrist, Eric Strauss. I took some of the patients' paintings to show him at the then new department of psychological medicine at St Bartholomew's Hospital. He was interested and suggested that I could go further into the psychodynamics of art by having some personal analysis and arranged for me to have weekly sessions with a Freudian psychiatrist, J.F. Lovel Barnes. Later, when I could afford it, I continued to use this invaluable opportunity by going to see him privately in Harley Street.

In this way I came to understand through myself the importance of transcribing sensuous, emotional and intuitive experiences into conscious thoughts, and the difficulties, benefits and limitations of words for communicating these thoughts to others. I made very few drawings and paintings as a direct contribution to my analytic work, and although I did a great deal of poetry and spontaneous writing that was helpful to me, I did not think of it as therapy. As my creative writing developed through analysis it gave me greater rapport with my patients and I felt free to read more. When I came across the remark in Freud's *Autobiographical Study* (Freud 1948: 119) that 'analysis can do nothing towards elucidating the nature of the artistic gift, nor can it explain the means by which the artist works', I suddenly felt elated: as one of those to whom Freud had addressed himself I was free to explore these problems and must do so if I was to develop my intuition that creative work was therapeutic in itself. In short, my need was less to know what I could do for patients than to know what they were doing for themselves and, incidentally, what I was doing for myself by creating art.

As I was not teaching art I was free to enjoy the variety of ways that patients used in handling paint and clay. Some people continued with one way of working for a long time then changed their style little by little, or suddenly altered it without an obvious reason. The subject matter was usually less varied than the styles, which might come in starts and stops. There were some efforts to mix a particular colour or draw a special sort of line but equally, there was a great deal of free improvization upon the work already made or with the original colour of the paper, or the accidental shape of the clay. Overpainting might completely transform the earlier work. Such changes might not necessarily appear in the finished work but would be hidden under layers of paint. I thought about my own work and the imaginative processes that brought it about: these were obviously more complicated than I had realized. Although I had learned to recognize the work of many famous artists by the style of their brushwork, it was only when I sat and watched patients painting that I realized that an artist's spontaneous posture and gestures are as much a part of his finished work as his ideas and feelings about the subject matter.

The physical, here-and-now aspect of art work provided the link between the art session and its beneficial effect. The session provided time for painting without direction or intention so the patients were free to be themselves, both in body and mind, and this included the freedom to change. The quality of each self-expression was shown in the unconscious style that the patient adopted, and change was recorded by alterations in his style. Their spontaneity and creative freedom reminded me of children's art although some patients reached beyond such simple, geometric shapes and colours and produced work that was closer to conventional art forms.

It was only when I had the temerity to empty all the patients' folders on to the floor one day and to look at the work divorced from all knowledge of its origin that I began to see a pattern emerging that could have some general application. It became clear that the strong, authoritative works that I had associated with patients' art had overshadowed another style that could be equally original but was tentative, or muted in colour and tone, and smaller in scale. The strong stuff, with its bold colours and large, simple shapes I called Archaic art and the other tentative or delicate work I called Traditional art as it seemed allied to the post-Renaissance tradition. I sorted several hundred works into these styles, and as I did so saw that each style could be subdivided into those dominated by lines or outlines of flat masses, and those that used colours and tones that suggested solid shapes. I gave descriptive names to these styles – the Archaic Linear style, the Archaic Massive style, the Traditional Linear style and the Traditional Massive style (Plates 1.1, 1.2, 1.3 and 1.4). Not every painting could be accounted for in this way, for there were a number that seemed to contain two, or even occasionally three, styles. This was bewildering at first, but eventually brought to light a very important aspect of their therapeutic value. I came to see that the styles bore an important relation to each other, some could appear together in one painting while others could not. Thus the two Archaic styles could appear together in one painting, and the same was true for the Traditional styles. The two Linear and the two Massive styles might also appear together and could flow into one another. However, the Archaic Linear and the Traditional Massive styles could not be integrated within a single work, and this limitation also applied to Archaic Massive with the Traditional Linear. It seemed that in these cases one style conflicted with the value system of the other. The relationship between the styles can be expressed diagrammatically (Figure 1.1). A painting might embody one basic style on its own or it might include elements from one of the adjacent styles, but a style evidently could not blend with one that was diametrically opposite.

The importance of the basic styles and the areas of transition in art as a therapy form the main theme of this book, and we shall return to the diagram repeatedly. However, before discussing it further I must digress to mention that the idea of a circular, rather than a linear arrangement of Archaic and Traditional styles brought to mind an arrangement that Jung presents in terms of more and less differentiated aspects of psychological types (Jung 1963: 60). In particular, he calls attention to the incompatibility between types on the opposite sides of the circle. His arrangement shows one dominant, or most differentiated, type associated with two less differentiated ones, the fourth type being the least accessible to a particular individual. He named the four types as the Sensation type, the Feeling type, the Intuitive type and the Thinking type. Much of this seemed to coincide with my ideas, and when I tried to fit the pictorial styles into the category of psychological types I was at first led to the obvious similarity between a thinking personality and the Traditional Linear style in which an artist plans, or first sketches out his work in an orderly fashion. The assured and generous gestures that go to make the Archaic Linear style seemed to express an exceptional sensitivity to sensuous awareness of body space, movement and kinaesthetic awareness generally. Brilliant, heavy masses of colour/tone certainly express an artist's emotions. The Traditional Massive style, which suggested form in space, might link with intuitions about the nature of external reality – and so with Jung's Intuitive types. I wondered if the idea of differentiation could account for consciously adopted, but habitual, prejudices. Thus, for instance, perhaps my own comparative in-difference to the value of Traditional Linear art was due to the fact that this style had been denigrated in my student days. My lack of 'differentiation' might have been caused by the association of this style with the Victorian romantic art movement which my generation felt itself to have outgrown. However, on the whole I felt that the idea of styles representing psycho-logical types was dangerously Procrustean, and I put aside the question for some years.

My attention was now caught by the complexity of the areas of overlap, or transition, as I came to see them. Patients whose art style could change seemed more creative as artists and to carry over this ability in their attitude to life: they were less rigid and fixed towards their symptoms also. More-over, when I compared these transitional paintings I could see that although some of them only showed elements of a second style, others had features that were quite unique. These features were not entirely limited to the aesthetic qualities of colour, scale and so on but consistently presented subjects in a chaotic, or a magical, or a literal or a schematic way. I found these transitional qualities very difficult to grasp but they forced me to extend my concept of styles from four to eight – four basic styles and four transitional ones (Figure 1.1).

When I talked to doctors about art styles I found that they were usually inclined to view them simply in terms of aesthetics, but one or two began to press me to find links between styles and psychiatric symptoms. Although there were some indications of such a relation they were not consistent and, moreover, the styles were not only found in patients' art but could be found in the arts as a whole. Thus many depressed people used the Traditional Massive style, which was impressionistic, but one could not diagnose the Impressionist movement as depressive. I was not trained to look for psychopathology and felt that any attempt of mine, however carefully supervised, would interfere with the patients' freedom of expression. As it was, the extent to which a patient used his art to express inner fantasies or his perception of the outer world seemed his affair: my task seemed simply to receive what he did on the level on which it was given.

By now I was seeing many different types of patient: physically and mentally ill people, children and adults, handicapped and disabled who had to live with damaged or deformed bodies. Their particular use of art seemed to reflect the way they saw their illness, and this might remain constant or change. A change in art style, rather than a change in subject seemed to come unintentionally, unnoticed or accepted as a 'happy accident'. I doubted whether a style could be changed deliberately: mannerisms might be temporarily adopted from another style, but they were not maintained, being swept away by the creative impulse. Change came through a spontaneous response to the art materials – an openness to colours, tones or shapes that had not been there before. I noticed that the basic styles were frequently used by chronically ill or disabled people, while the transitional styles more usually expressed states of acute illness (Hamilton and Simon 1980 and McCourt *et al.* 1984).

Children's art styles seemed a different matter: they reflected the level of maturation rather than the age of the child (Simon 1976). Generally, the Archaic styles of young children continued with little change for five or six years, the Traditional elements being limited to the last year or two of childhood. A young child was usually unable to use the style of an older child, although the reverse was often true. Maturation seemed to follow the circle of styles in a clockwise direction starting from the Archaic Linear and sometimes missing out one style or another, but an anticlockwise movement was also possible (Figure 1.1); that is, from the Archaic Linear style to the Traditional Linear where it halted. This phenomenon rarely appeared before age five, in my experience. However, there was also a third form of movement in styles – a loop going back and forward again. I was seized by the idea of 'reculer pour mieux sauter' (Koestler, 1970: 173), and the thought that for some people art as a therapy might be a temporary return to an earlier stage that had been missed, or upset at its proper time. For such people their use of creative art might demand a 'regression in service of the Ego' (Kris 1973: 177) that was even comparable to the transference neurosis discovered in psychoanalysis. 'Inartistic' people might need to resume the style that they had used when they had been active creatively, perhaps long ago, in childhood.

By the 1960s I had returned to the idea of styles as a mirror of personality, but in terms of habitual moods or attitudes rather than consistent personality types. It seemed that these attitudes were projected unconsciously as a way of seeing life. The attitude was reflected in the way the art was imaged – its style. A patient's style helped me to understand his underlying mood, something that might not be seen in any other way.

I had now to find some names or descriptive terms for the attitudes that were reflected in the styles. Terms such as Archaic Massive gave no indication of the underlying psychological meaning and I could not wholly accept Jung's formulation of Sensation, Feeling, Intuition and Thought although they were tantalizingly close to the terminology I wanted. The Traditional styles certainly reflected thought and intuition, although intuition in art seemed insolubly linked with perception, but the Archaic styles did not altogether fit Jung's description of Sensation and Feeling types as I understood these terms. In the wide, ballet-like gestures that created the Archaic Linear style I found a sensuous response to life that might be sexually implicit or explicit and this quality of vivid, physical life was not indicated to me by the word 'sensation'. Sensation is an abstract term that does not reflect human experience. One might say that a patient, or an insect for that matter, can be observed in the studio as having sensations but when a human being paints and we see him using the Archaic Linear style then we see in the work an expression of the sensuous reality of life. My other difficulty was with Jung's classification of a Feeling type. Although his descriptions fitted the Archaic Massive style, I was bothered by the term itself, for although we feel emotion we also feel sensuous sometimes and can describe our intuitions and even our notions as feelings. Paintings in the Archaic Massive style have an emotional effect through the violence of their colours and the massive appearance of large forms. Patients who painted in this way assumed that their emotions were the only true guide to the reality of any situation, and that any other view was misguided or false. Indeed any of the attitudes carries a basic assumption that it is the only real and true one during the time that it is held; consequently a consistent change in style indicates a radical change in the patient's grasp of reality. I have therefore used the idea of *feelings* to indicate the general area of sensuous, emotional and intuitive perceptions, and limited the meaning of the Archaic Massive style to the portrayal of emotion.

After 1968 I felt reasonably confident that I could summarize my idea that moods or attitudes to life are reflected in the four basic styles of art. I saw the Archaic Linear style expressing the sensuous life of the body, that D.H. Lawrence (1990) has described as being 'alone within my skin, which is the walls of all my domain'. The Archaic Massive style elaborates this attitude with emotional judgements of right and wrong. Both styles are dominated by subjective, ('haptic', Lowenfeld 1965), experiences. The Traditional styles refer to the external world; the Traditional Massive style reflecting the artist's intuitive perceptions and the Traditional Linear style defining appearances through their factual and logical meanings. The areas of transition between two adjacent styles reflect the degree to which they can be held simultaneously. The four attitudes reflected in the basic styles can be shown in a diagram similar to Figure 1.1.

My interest in the psychophysical aspect of art led me to observe differences in quality appearing in the earliest scribbles that little children make. I had noticed differences in my own children's drawings and paintings and also in my friend's little children. In 1983 I arranged some 'Mother and toddler paint and play groups' at the Open College in Belfast and held

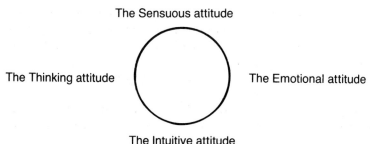

The Sensuous attitude

The Thinking attitude

The Emotional attitude

The Intuitive attitude

school-holiday groups for some older children in my own studio. As art work is so intimately bound up with posture and gesture I wondered if the high rate of failure in art at puberty was in part due to the drastic physiological changes that were taking place then.

As might be expected, children's art styles normally reflect the level of their maturation, regardless of their chronological age. However, they also show the overriding influence of the content of the work, which is affected by the child's mood and his subject matter (Simon 1976). Although Archaic styles are generally used until puberty, some Traditional elements occur during latency in a Massive transitional form. Most young children are unable to use the style of an older child but there are a few exceptions, such as Nadia (Selfe 1977) and those who do not work spontaneously but have learnt a stereotype from an older child. Maturation, starting from the Archaic Linear style normally progresses in a clockwise direction but some children with early emotional difficulties may develop a style that moves anti-clockwise, towards the Traditional Linear or even, as in the case of Nadia to Traditional Massive representations of form in space.

All these experiences gave me a wide view of the different ways that children respond creatively to an opportunity to make things by themselves if they can have an adult audience to hold the situation safely. In an open area like this, play is therapy, and when I saw how naturally creative impulses moved the children from one art material to another my ideas about art therapy with adults was extended. These half-coordinated ideas about the similarity of adult and child art became a sudden revelation when I was fortunate enough to meet Sister Leonie Bowland while organizing an introductory course on art therapy in Dublin in 1981. I saw her remarkable collection of drawings by children aged three and four that had been done while they were waiting at a clinic for their mothers, who were in therapy. Sister Leonie had originally intended only to occupy the children while they were waiting but, seeing so many drawings together, she had become fascinated by the feelings they conveyed. When I saw them I was immediately struck by their similarity to adult works in the Archaic Linear style and could see that the art work of children offered a means to understand a universal language of symbolic images. This was not a dead language from prehistory or the eccentric doodles of secluded psychiatric patients, but a spontaneous form of communication used by all active, lively children, who freely developed their fantasies in all kinds of art work and dramatic play. These works expressed, in various ways, the need to create a containing shape for the artist to be himself, which, in turn, could fit into a shape that was distinct from himself.

This pattern of shapes, that I call the Circle in the Square, has a particular effect upon the artist. His behaviour shows a sense of achievement: he looks relaxed and satisfied. He may say he is triumphant, or happy, or quietly satisfied. He may notice his change of mood and feel surprised that his headache or weariness has gone. He may describe his feelings as 'coming together, inside', or being rested, or well fed – a description that reminded me that children often model food that has a circular shape: pies filled with plums, buns and biscuits, eggs and hamburgers. Descriptions of this sense of satisfaction may be volunteered by adults or children and by anyone who uses free, spontaneous art work, not only by patients suffering mental stress. I could see that creative art is invigorating and that it draws from the artist a sense of his own integrity, an actual, physical sense of being sound, entirely and honestly combined into a whole. Nothing I could do or say seemed to be as important as this discovery of the patient's self and as it came from the actual work process I realized that I must accept the validity of all spontaneous art in its different styles of presentation, and try to observe the moment when a patient begins to elaborate his unthinking gestures with fantasies that would include the Circle, or impose a rational idea upon his work. No style could be thought pathological in itself, although an exclusive use of one style in spontaneous work could be excessively self-limiting; for such a person even the ordinary contingencies of life might seem a threat. However, I could not change the patient's unconscious attitude even if I drew his attention to it. The best I could do was to provide a situation in which he had an opportunity to express himself freely in art and might accept and use any changes that occurred in his style. When I had become familiar with the meaning of the art styles I could sometimes help a patient who was feeling blocked by tuning to the attitude that was expressed in his style; this allowed me to respond more appropriately. When art is the therapy of choice, non-verbal communication between therapist and patient has priority.

Eventually I came to identify the Circle in the Square with a universal need to create a symbolic image that integrates the split we make in reality when we differentiate between things inside and outside ourselves. From patients' work I realized that our need to make such an image is with us throughout life and may be in us long before we can scribble. Yet these symbolic images are not permanent, they need to be rediscovered, recreated, time and again. Their importance lies beyond the object created; the value of art work lies chiefly in the opportunity it gives to experience creative initiative. It is the doing, rather than what is done which can reward us with the sense of being whole psychophysical beings acting in relation to both inner and outer reality. The moment of integration is imaged in the shape of a circle in a square. At this point my previous observations about styles fell into place as four basically different ways of elaborating the basic symbol in terms of a person's dominant attitude to life.

Chapter 1

The theory of styles

A picture can be appreciated from two points of view. It can arouse interest in its content and it can speak to us through its style; the way in which the representation or abstraction is painted makes an essential contribution to its meaning. Although style and content are actually indivisible in the painting itself and in the mind of the painter during its construction they are not one and the same for they connote different aspects of the creative process.

The immediate mood of the painter influences his choice of subject and has an important effect upon the pictorial content. Changes of mood may occur as a painting develops and the final mood at its completion does much to determine any discussion between patient and therapist. Such transitory moods do not, however, generally affect a person's habitual style. His unthinking way of handling an art material reflects his habitual attitude towards life.

Memories, emotions, sensations and ideas that a patient may wish to communicate or exclude also help determine the pictorial content. Content, as I am using the term, is not only a result of the painter's conscious intention, shown in the subject matter, title and art form, but also has a latent aspect which may only occur to the artist intermittently during the process of creation and be forgotten or surpressed by the time the work is completed. Psychotherapies that are primarily concerned with verbal communication between patient and therapist are naturally focused upon the content of completed art work; however, if a patient does not or cannot talk about his work, its latent content is not available, and any meaning that appears to lie below the surface remains ambiguous unless subject to the therapist's interpretation. The therapist cannot discuss the content of a patient's work unaided, even though it may seem recognizable in terms of familiar fantasies or general clinical experience. Such an interpretation, offered to a patient, might have some general validity and yet be very far from his particular or immediate needs and therefore unusable or even damaging to therapeutic progress by limiting the patient's attention to the content or subject matter and leading him to consider art as a pictographic communication, or a substitute for verbalization of the psychological problem.

An art therapist's understanding of art styles is necessary for understanding a patient's whole personality, including his problem, within the wider structure of his total being. The habitual style is as much a physiological as a psychological form of expression; it reflects his muscular and perceptual responses as well as his assumptions and unconsidered habits of thought. Any work in a different style from his usual one reflects a powerful change of mood. Naturally, until we have several paintings from a patient we cannot assess his habitual attitude. Nevertheless, I have found that from the first session, and before there has been time to establish a therapeutic relationship, the pictorial style offers a wealth of meaning to the therapist and, as the work continues, the style monitors changes that are taking place in the depths of the patient's personality.

Our understanding of the content is not diminished by the study of the patient's style; rather, it is enriched. The style determines the attitude of the painter towards his subject: some subjects are enhanced by the style and others diminished by it.

THE CIRCLE OF STYLES

Styles in art can be divided into four basic types. Figure 1.1 shows how the relation between them creates a circular system; the basic styles are shown in capital letters.

In some works a particular style is used throughout and may be continued as the usual or habitual style of the artist. However, there are other works that show two or even three styles that are associated together in the circle, and the artist's subsequent paintings may move between them. There is also the occasional painting in which a style is almost consistent but one part of the picture may be totally different, indicating a radical change of mood. All the styles may be seen in the spontaneous work of adults and children up to puberty. Two of the styles are Archaic, which is to say that they have an appearance of primitive or prehistoric art, and the other two styles are familiar to us in works made in the post-Renaissance tradition of representation. Between these basic styles there are areas of overlap that I term areas of transition. In these any art work may show more or less of the qualities of a basic style. In each of the transitions there may develop some original features not seen in either of the contributing basic styles; these indicate conflict between the attitudes underlying the adjoining styles. I discuss these transitional styles in a subsection of this chapter, but at this point I will describe the typical features of each basic style. The illustrative examples are: Plates 1.1, 1.2, 1.3 and 1.4.

Plate 1.1 is an example of the Archaic Linear style. It is perhaps the most immediately impressive style, for the scale is huge, giving a grand effect to

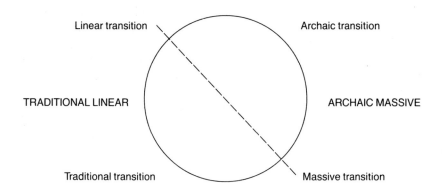

Figure 1.1 The circle of styles

Four basic styles of art are recognized: they are located at four points of the compass and are indicated in the diagram by capital letters. These styles are linked by transitional areas in which there is generally an overlap of the character-istic features of the adjacent areas. This overlap in the properties of the adjacent areas creates four transitional styles making eight styles in all.

Some art works use only one style: others contain more than one. Movement from one style to another is generally in a clockwise direction, although during therapy there may be some anticlockwise movement.

Two basic styles are Archaic and two are Traditional. The division lies diagon-ally in the position indicated by a dotted line.

Children's art usually starts at the Archaic Linear position and develops clock-wise round the circle. In Western cultural tradition continuity is broken during latency when further change would overlap the original Archaic Linear style.

work that may be quite small in actual size. The shapes are simple, geometric and symmetrical and colours are flat, heraldic and in contrast to the outline. The artist is carried by his sensuous rapport with the material and a sense of physical coordination within his whole body. He can paint a circle with a single sweep of the brush and draws a straight line without mechanical aid.

Plate 1.2 is an example of the Archaic Massive style. It is also huge in scale but the outlines are less evident, being lost and found within brilliant areas of colour that work together by contrast so that the whole painting seems to vibrate. The artist's sense of colour is so acute that he is con-tinually aware of the effect of one colour upon another and frequently changes or modifies them by some overpainting that may extend the original outlines and give the shapes an impression of convexity – sometimes even as if they press up from the pictorial surface. The picture has not the elegance of Archaic Linear art but the artist works with bold assurance.

Plate 1.3 shows the typical appearance of the Traditional Massive style. In this the scale is greatly reduced and small details appear to recede into space. The colours are diffused to give an all-over effect of light and the brushwork is tentative: short strokes or cross-hatching usually being preferred. The work is visualized as a whole, each part being affected by the rest.

Plate 1.4 presents a version of the Traditional Linear style. Here we can see small scale used to define the factual appearance of objects presented in the subject matter. To this end, line is emphasized and colour limited within the clear boundary of the outline. Although geometric perspective is used, it does not give an effect of recession, only the idea of it. The artist's posture and gestures are stiff, being dominated by the small muscles of his hand and eye. He plans his work, tends to use mechanical aids, and works methodically.

TRANSITIONAL STYLES

The areas of overlap between styles that I have defined as transitional may show a harmonious blend of two adjacent styles in which there is more of one style than the other. However, there are some paintings in which both styles appear to conflict and, as a result, throw up a particular quality that strongly overcasts any subject matter. For this reason I have described these art works as made in a Transitional Style to distinguish them from those showing a simple combination of adjacent styles. Each Transitional Style will be illustrated in its relevant chapter.

The Archaic Transitional Style is marked by the chaotic effect: line and mass are present separately as unrelated scribbles, smears and blots. Any image or theme is fragmented. The Massive Transitional Style shows discordance between the large scale of Archaic art and the small scale of the Traditional: consequently the work appears clumsy, for large movements are being employed to indicate small details. The subject matter is distinctive; animistic and anthropomorphic images abound, animals have a human appearance and people are often grotesque, like the little people of fairy tales. The effect of the Traditional Transitional Style is opposite to this effect for the images are clearly defined and skilfully presented in an idealized way: shapes and colours are distinctive and immaculate. However, this perfectionism may be superficial and gives the unnatural effect of mannerism. A similar emphasis on definition invades the Linear Transitional Style together with the literal and factual appearance of Traditional Linear art; as a result many of these paintings use some sort of pictographic shorthand, words, letters or numbers may be included in a conventional representation.

STYLE AND CONTENT

The art style gives meaning to the subject matter, drawing on our associations to fill out the content of the work. A flower painting in the Archaic Massive style (Figure 4.7) may remind us of the voluptuousness of flowers, their colour, even their weight and perfume rather than their delicacy and impermanence. Likewise, a cup painted in the Archaic Linear style will indicate its significance as a sacred vessel (Figure 5.3) that would be seen only as a drinking vessel if presented as one detail in a Traditional painting. Many paintings show conflict through their transitional style, or a partial integration of two different views of the subject. An example of the first might be seen in Figure 2.1, where a Traditional Linear architectural drawing has become muddled by heavy Archaic Massive colouring. In this work the two styles are utterly opposed. Partial integration is seen in the delicate seascape painted in a Massive Transitional style (Figure 7.3). In this picture a mainly Traditional Massive painting includes a few details in larger scale. On the whole, the content is more verbally accessible in the Traditional than in the Archaic styles; there are many conscious associations, both added as visual images and also developed by the artist as stories or reminiscences arising from later contemplation of his work. By comparison, the formal simplicity of the Archaic style may seem deceptively empty of content only because there is little to say about it. For this reason alone it is very important to realize that the style of a work is the symbolic image of the artist's unconscious attitude to his life at that particular time, and may indeed be the habitual, pervasive condition of his mental distress. In this sense the style forms a part of unconscious content which may include repression or a long-held resistance directed against some inner or outer stimuli.

No style is pathological in itself; however, it may be put to ill use if it reflects a fixed and habitual attitude that overrides the essential needs of the artist and his environment. A patient, coming to use art as therapy, showing a fixed, inflexible style in a variety of subjects cannot alter his style until he works spontaneously. This is extremely hard for him and, at first, changes may be very small. These new growths need delicate handling, left *in situ* until they have developed in their own time. Patients who suffer such anxious rigidity in style are all too ready to denigrate such changes as accidents or failures of some sort: the changes easily cause alarm because they indicate a deep shift in the sense of reality. For example, a patient who is totally committed to the idea of reality as factual, measurable or logical, will feel that any intuitive responses are merely guesses or logical weaknesses. Or, the patient who depends upon the strength of his emotions to measure the reality of his experiences will be inclined to deprecate his sensuous life as 'cold' sensuality. Only a patient's sense of security in the therapeutic milieu can hold these self-criticisms in check. He must be able to feel himself to be real, both by staying the same and also by changing in his own good time.

Change may proceed round the circle of styles in a clockwise direction, sensuous reality being enriched by emotional values, which are in turn refined and broadened by the subtleties of intuitive perceptions of the outer world. On the other hand, a patient's oppressive sense of the relativity of all things may be given direction by conceptual frames of thought, which in turn are enriched by a sensuous awareness of the actual, guiding and limiting abstract thought. At any point in the circle a patient may enter and move spontaneously towards another style. If the move is in the form of a jump across the circle, the underlying mood will be too disturbed to consolidate the style in one painting; however, if we compare work in a sequence of paintings such as Plates 7.1 to 7.6 and 8.1 to 8.6, there may be a very wide range of styles, suggesting an extensive alteration in a patient's attitude; movement here was not always clockwise but also showed some temporary regressions before moving forward again. In such cases, where a patient has worked for some time in therapy with art, movement may be from the Traditional to the Archaic, or vice versa; in either case the patient is claiming a part of reality that was previously unavailable to him. Through the symbolic imagery of art he has used sensuous, emotional, intuitive, or conceptual reality, even though he may have been cut off from one or more of these in other areas of his life in the past.

Creative art is not a cure-all: if it were, no artist would go mad. However, art as therapy does offer troubled people an opportunity to discover their creative initiative towards life through the symbolic imagery of art. So often it seems that the wonderful potential of the child's grasp of life is lost in the strictures of his adult condition. At first a patient can often only re-create art but, in effect, to copy art is to copy life. This attitude to art indicates that he sees himself as a creation of others, or of fate. As he continues to use the therapeutic hour, he recovers the sense of autonomous life. His work may not focus upon his immediate problems, or even bring conscious insights into their underlying cause but I think that insight does occur although, like a dream, it may be lost to consciousness as the creative work comes to an end. I do not think that this is altogether a bad thing, for understanding, if it becomes fully conscious, is only a part of mental life. Moreover, many patients recall such lost meanings when they look back over their old work. What we are belongs under what we do.

In summary, this chapter has attempted to describe a general framework in which therapeutic change can be recognized in a patient's art work. Within such a frame there are many individual variations – the creativity of each one of us continually extends beyond any theoretical formulation.

Figure 2.1 *Hospital* Traditional Linear

Chapter 2

The use of style in crisis intervention

I have chosen to introduce an example of the value of understanding art styles in a brief case in which three paintings (Figures 2.2, 2.3, 2.4) were made in the first of four sessions. The patient did not paint again but used these paintings extensively in working through his immediate problem. Although the brevity of this case is not at all typical of my work, I think that it gives a rather clear view of the richness of communication that art work provides when the style is understood to reflect the patient's unconscious attitude. I believe that without the opportunity to make these paintings in my sight the patient might have been stuck in a malignant pattern of illness and role of patient.

I had met Christopher socially on a couple of occasions but I did not think that he knew about my hospital work. However, he made an appointment to see me at my home and there told me that he had become ill about two months before, suffering extreme anxiety and sleeplessness. When his mother had sought medical help he had been admitted as a voluntary patient and given eight electro-convulsive treatments and a course of tranquillizers. After two weeks at home he had developed more symptoms and had come to me as an alternative to another admission to hospital. I was rather unsure about the advisability of taking him on and possibly delaying further treatment that might help him but he seemed to hope that he could work with me, and it proved successful.

Chris described his state as being intolerably fearful, afraid of travelling and even of being out of doors at all. He described delusional ideas about family members and complained of tremors in his hands and mouth. During the interview he was very restless, rocking on his chair or pacing the room. He frequently bent himself over as if in pain and covered his face with his hands. Occasionally he seemed near to tears and several times intense, embarrassed laughter burst from him. His memory for past events was perfectly clear but his account was confusing when he tried to describe the present. Chris imagined that the cause of his tension was overwork during a stay abroad. After leaving university he had roamed the world for two years, visiting many different countries in which he had a variety of temporary jobs. While working very hard on a foreign television series he was one of an intimate trio with another man and a girl. He described them as not really his type but said that they were forced into each other's company by the lack of social life. He was rather inclined to think that the complications of a situation in which two men shared the attention of one girl might possibly have added to the strain. He reported, rather casually, that the girl had enjoyed heavy petting and that she had led him to the point of intercourse on three occasions, to refuse him at the last minute. When I asked him how he had dealt with his feelings about this he said that there was no question of an alternative satisfaction. He commented that, looking back on it, it seemed that she had been rather cruel. The patient then confided to me that he had begun to believe that he was becoming homosexual. He was now afraid to travel by train in case he might make overtures to a man although, he said, that if a man accosted him he would hit him between the eyes. Chris also confided that he had recently concluded that his father was a latent homosexual. In response to my offer to discuss these matters after he had made some paintings he became calmer and expressed doubts about his intellectual honesty, going on to describe early masturbation rituals and other guilt-laden fantasies. He agreed to return in a couple of days and paint, as he had already some feeling of relief from confiding in me and was terrified of the idea that he might go mad.

At this stage, the patient had a little understanding of himself. He was aware that the triangular affair might have some significance, but he was unable to realize any depth of feeling for the man or the girl. His mention of intellectual honesty indicated that he suspected that his illness had some hidden advantage, but there was nothing to indicate that this suspicion was strong enough to prevent him from becoming more and more absorbed in the delusion of becoming homosexual. I wondered whether I should persuade him to return to hospital as there was a possibility that he might become entangled with the law, or even commit suicide, so great was his anguish. However, as I felt that we had established a good rapport I decided to postpone the decision until he had made some paintings.

When Chris arrived for the painting session he said he was terrified. He looked very tense, breathing quickly and sighing. First he showed me a sketch (Figure 2.1) he had made some weeks before, while in hospital. This had begun as a conventional brush drawing of the hospital building and gardens but he had overpainted it in a way that distorted the perspective, making it almost unintelligible. Chris told me that he was not in the habit of painting but he did have art materials and also his guitar with him during his hospital stay.

When Christ had shown me this painting he was able to sit down and use the art materials to make a quick brush drawing of a guitar player (Figure 2.2). He seemed to use the colour in a random way, having more than one on his brush at a time. First he drew a domed square in black at the

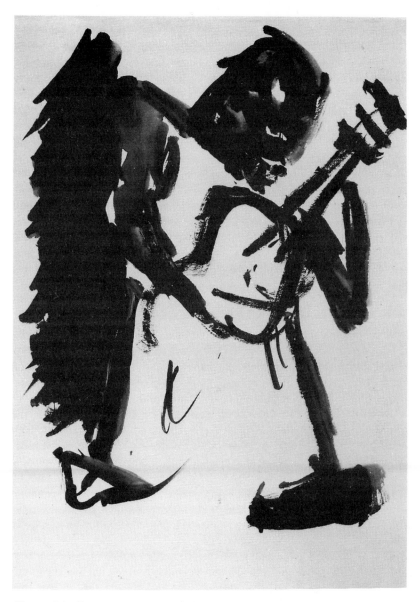

Figure 2.2 *Guitar player* Massive Transition

top of the paper, set diagonally at the same angle as the neck of the guitar which was incompletely drawn in black. Then he filled in a black area on the left side and also the face area with clumsy strokes which were so violently overworked that it was impossible to follow the representation. Finally, he used blue to outline the left arm and leg and, dipping his brush in yellow paint, he overpainted the wet blue, transforming most of it into green. He used this colour to add some lines to the right side of the figure. The effect was of a squat, demon-like figure, strongly lit from the front and casting a black shadow on the left. Two triangles at the bottom of the picture might have been intended as footlights but they also gave an impression of being attached to the legs – like the blocks that are given to amputees when they first begin to walk. The work is in the Massive Transition: many features referring to the Archaic Massive style – the large scale, vitality and sense of solid mass. I was also aware of the effect of lighting, suggesting some spontaneous recollection of an actual stage coming from perceptual memory rather than the emotional state expressed by the painting as a whole. This effect of powerful lighting obliterated the division between the musician's legs.

As Chris passed the work to me he said, miserably, 'It could be anyone, man or woman, could be me ... probably is! Rather silly, the arm has two joints ... I'm afraid you will see me – queer. Last time I told you everything ... woke up with the sun on my back door ... now I've told you everything – coming here, I feel ...' As he did not continue speaking I told Chris that I did not want to talk about this picture until he had painted as much as he could, and I handed him another sheet of paper. He began to paint again, using clear colours and a clean brush to make a huge head (Figure 2.3). First, he painted two clear yellow shapes as eyes and filled in the area above them with brilliant red, giving an impression of hair. He added a diagonal line with black paint for the nose, and curving lines for the mouth and chin. The base of the page was painted, with black, and the pupils of the eyes added with black also. His manner changed a good deal as he worked; the muddled, agitated scribbling gave way to precise shaping of features with large, skilful strokes. Chris seemed intensely focused upon the painting, withdrawn and unable to speak. He studied it for some time before handing it to me. Without comment I handed fresh paper to him again and he rapidly daubed at it with strokes of red, green and dull shades of orange/yellow, surrounding this with a black rectangle radiating grey/black lines (Figure 2.4). Then he leaned away from the table, saying that he was quite exhausted.

After a little rest I complimented Chris on his wholehearted response, and we were able to discuss the content of the paintings. Referring to the *Guitar player*, I pointed out that, although he was afraid that this painting would show him as a 'queer', that is, confirming his homosexuality, in fact it only underlined his doubts, for the space between the legs was empty as he faced questions about his sexual identity and the meaning of the homosexual fantasies. He found this idea encouraging. Then we turned to the painting of the face. He identified it as a portrait of the girlfriend and looked at it carefully again, remarking, 'She certainly looks through ... the red is her good side, her vivacity; the black is her ... what I think she may be, but I

Figure 2.3 *The witch girl* Archaic Massive

Figure 2.4 *Lysistrata* Traditional Linear

don't know, so it doesn't go right down to the bottom of the page.... I don't really blame her, for she has had a very unsettled life.'

Such an intuitive mood, giving rise to an expression of sympathy seemed to obscure the actual emotional impact of the picture. It seemed to me an attempt to rationalize feelings that had been conscious at the time of painting. I responded to the communication given by the Archaic Massive style of the painting in my reply: 'But you have painted a witch who has stolen your manhood – can someone do that, do you think?' Chris looked frightened and said violently, 'I damn well hope not.' I asked him again, 'Do you believe that someone could do that, could so dominate another person as to cast a spell on him and take his manhood away?'

Then Chris became very agitated and moved about in the same sort of way that he had done on the first visit, showing the panic of his helplessness; however, we were able to link his homosexual fantasies to his need to escape from his dependence on the frustrating 'witch girl'. As he came to recognize the strength of his infantile terror he was able to recall positive feelings towards both friends, and his grief when both the man and the girl deceived him. His suggestibility and anxiety in the session gave way to a relaxed and rather companionable attitude and he turned to his last painting (Figure 2.4) and offered to interpret it to me, saying;

> Well, in that case the next painting will be meaningful. It represents a stage set for the play *Lysistrata*. I was looking through some slides before I came tonight and I saw some that I had made of the production. You know, the play is about some Greek women who refuse their husbands.... I wanted to leave some paper white.

I asked Chris which were the red lines that show distinctly against the white background. 'Either the men or the women. I had to keep them separate, so I put in a yellow background.'

DISCUSSION OF THE ART WORK

When considering the significance of Chris's paintings in terms of the subject and style we see that he only offered four paintings in all and that in these he only represented three of the eight styles that may be used. The styles that he did not use inform us as much as those that he did use. For instance, why did this young man not paint in the Traditional Massive style that one would have expected from such a gentle and sensitive person, one whose empathy with his girlfriend led him to say 'I really don't blame her, for she had a very unsettled life'? Had he made more paintings, some of them might have reflected the intuitive/perceptive quality of this side of him, but they were not apparent at the time that he was reaching out for therapeutic help. In comparison, these paintings appeared regressed and I hoped that this was a sign of therapeutic regression. From the picture that he brought with him I could see that the styles moved from the intellectual position of a clever young man who had made a conventional, architectural type of sketch from sight and then messed it up in the painting. This painting showed the failure of his Traditional Linear approach and seemed to indicate that the doubt he expressed about his intellectual honesty at the end of our first meeting was a truthful and accurate statement about a false rationalization he was adopting towards his former friends. In the light of his hospital picture, his undoubted intelligence would have allowed him to learn and adopt a rational attitude, but, like the perspective drawing, he could not carry it off when he was faced with a need to use colour – which depended upon an emotional response. Moreover, geometric perspective could not indicate recessive space without an intuitive sense of relationship through tone. Thus my personal disquiet about his lack of feeling about the 'rather cruel' behaviour of the girlfriend seemed confirmed by the characteristics of the art style of the work. I might guess that this failure of his self-esteem, when his dominant attitude of thinking threatened to desert him caused his panic anxiety as a crisis of identity. He was really afraid that he was not the brilliant young man who had scored high on the Mensa test because his intellectual equipment could not replace his emotional impoverishment. All this I could surmise from his first painting, together with the things he had told me, but I did not know how he was to recover himself.

The next painting showed the direction of his therapeutic impulse. The subject of a guitarist showed another aspect of himself as a musician, rather than an architect, but this painting also showed his conflict, for he felt that the figure was a 'queer', perhaps by long hair that hides his face and a gap where his genitals would be indicated. The style of painting was definitely Archaic, the scale was large and had all the characteristics of the Massive Transition. The colour, of yellowish green and black, gave a luridly dramatic and sinister effect, the brushwork was heavy and crude. Only the lighting indicated some naturalism. In this painting Chris's mood seemed dominated by the twilight of primitive, magical anthropomorphism.

When I handed Chris a fresh sheet of paper he started to paint again immediately, shaping the eyes with yellow paint and then adding the clear red area above, and finally the black below (Figure 2.3). This Archaic Massive picture was so full of life and energy and the Archaic scale of the image so huge that he could only fit the head and shoulders into the available space. The directness of this painting, its lack of overwork and the simple strength of the colour suggested some 'heraldic' association, and this was borne out by the remark he made later when, describing the work as a portrait of his girlfriend, he said, 'The red is her good side, her vivacity: the black is her ... what I think she may be, but I don't know, so it doesn't go right down to the bottom of the page....' From this it seemed that the area of the colours, as well as their shade had specific meaning for him. The lemon yellow diamond shapes of her eyes gave a hypnotic effect, typical of Archaic Linear images. Chris stared for some time at this picture, murmuring, 'She certainly looks through . . .'.

The final painting (Figure 2.4) shows another, unexpected change of mood, reflected in another change of style. In this, the Traditional Linear style, his gestures were more restrained: he used a smaller brush and thinner paint. The brush strokes were short and the work quickly made. As he sat looking at it he deliberately added some masses of colour round the separate strokes that softened their contrasts within the painted square. The total effect is diagrammatic and could not be understood without knowing that it came to refer to the theme of *Lysistrata* and the importance of distinguishing male and female roles.

When we reconsider the paintings in the light of their different styles it is possible to understand how Chris made use of painting as a self-therapy. First he showed his inability to contain his emotional needs within intellectual boundaries, and then *Guitar player* spoke of his need to meet the primitive world of psychic terrors and castration fears; also perhaps, his feeling of fraudulence in setting up to be the performer of a role. Only then was he free to express the violence of sensuous emotion that had been repressed in his dealings with the 'witch girl'. When that emotion became visible I intervened because, by his kindly assessment of her difficulties, I felt strongly that he was losing the opportunity to re-experience the full force of his emotion, and would escape once more into the intellectual dishonesty that, he felt, had claimed him before. His misplaced sympathy seemed an aspect of the disguised guitarist, spotlit on the stage of virile life, but perhaps only 'half there'. Fear of this cruel self-judgement seemed to have been at the back of his tremendous anxiety when he tried to leave medical care and resume normal life. His projection of sensuous and emotional reality upon the image of the 'witch girl' as a sexually attractive female invited the delusion that he was becoming homosexual; but once again the 'witch girl' saw through the sham when she stared out at him from his painting. This was the way that Chris found himself again, as far as I could see. His final painting appears to be a summing up of this insight in the form of the classic story of *Lysistrata* and its performance, in which he could identify his dilemma as a man who suffers at the hands of woman, and survives.

Some further mention should be made of the quality of my intervention during the withdrawn state that befell Chris after he had painted *The witch girl.* At that point I became concerned by the depth of his withdrawal and felt that it was high time to call back his sense of outer reality and use his critical intellect upon the dichotomy between the description he had given of the girl as a weak, misguided tease, and the hypnotic image in his painting. I did not know how he would resolve this but I felt that it was essential for him to realize fully that he himself had created the witch image. That is why I responded to the painting in its own dramatic terms, to reinforce the emotional violence that it displayed. This shocked him into an appraisal.

In speaking like this I was acting with concern for my own needs as well as those of my patient. I was taking into account the whole circumstances as I saw them, as well as his urgent need to stay out of hospital. In the long run it might have been better if he could have worked out his feelings slowly, step by step, as it were, rather than to leap forward into the safety of an intellectual solution. I would have preferred to work in this way with him. However, his symptoms disappeared in the following order: intense anxiety and depression lightened after the first session, fear of travel lifted immediately after the painting session and his homosexual delusion faded a week later. Chris did not want to paint again but used another two sessions to fill in gaps in his memory and understanding about the critical time before and during his breakdown. He reviewed many incidents that had added confusion to his damaged sense of identity and then went on to consider practical ways in which he could develop, now that he was getting better. Six weeks after the last therapy session, in a follow-up interview, he no longer showed physical symptoms of tension or complained of them but mentioned bouts of depression. Asked to describe these feelings he said that they only lasted a few hours and he thought that they were not excessive for someone who was still without suitable work and had no girlfriend. Seen briefly, a month or two after this, he looked very well, his movements were easy and he had lost the excess weight caused by the sedatives. The colour was back in his face and not long afterwards Chris found satisfying work on a newspaper and acquired two girls in two months. The first girl was as unsuitable as the 'witch girl' had been: although he had no psychotic reaction this time, the relationship aroused anxiety which, he said, made him feel isolated. He withdrew from this conflict and then met a friend from college days; they teamed up and he had plans to live with her and marry her eventually if 'they were not too serious-minded'.

SUMMARY

My responsiveness to the non-verbal meaning of a patient's art style enabled me to intervene rather strongly when he seemed inclined to fall into a downward spiral of mental symptoms as an escape from an intolerable threat to his sense of self. Although he would only paint during one session and only came for four therapeutic hours altogether, his wholehearted commitment during that time suggests that art as a therapy, used in this way can be claimed as a form of crisis intervention.

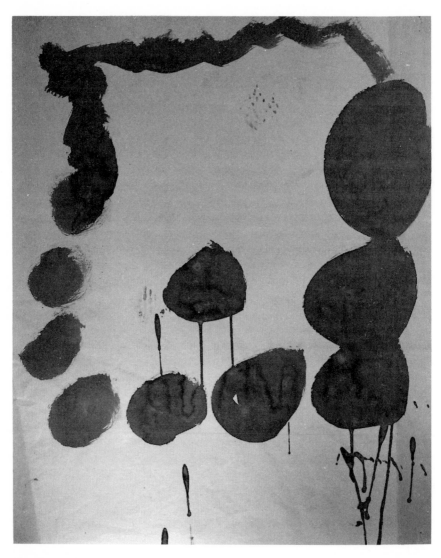

Figure 3.1 *Buns for everyone* Archaic Transition

Chapter 3

The development of styles in childhood

In the previous chapter I indicated that the style of an art work provides an important contribution to our understanding of the artist's unconscious attitude to his subject. The style may be habitual or the effect of a mood; for instance, each painting that Chris made was in a different style and this showed me how rapidly his mood could change according to the experiences he chose to illustrate. This heightened versatility gave him an unusual responsiveness to life and the flexibility that seems to have helped him over this difficult time, although it also caused him the extreme distress that brought out his confused sense of identity. The styles he used showed me his unconscious attitude towards the subject matter at a time when he was full of doubt about his intellectual honesty. Because his situation was so critical I chose to follow the unconscious communication of the styles rather than his confusing rationalizations.

In this chapter I shall compare children's art with the circle of styles, to develop the idea that there is a basic symbolic imagery that is fundamental to both adults and children. I am aware that mental growth is generally seen as a progression from less to more differentiated complex states. My idea of maturation in art follows a circular movement from Archaic to Traditional and has the potential for continuing in cyclic evolution through the circle of styles again.

THE CHANGING APPEARANCE OF CHILD ART

Children begin to draw or paint when they notice that their gestures are recorded in smears and scribbles. As early as the second year some babies enjoy this and want to repeat the experience. The marks show the child what he has done and therefore they are a valued means of self-communication before he has the words to frame thoughts and before the scribbles mean anything to anyone else.

Kellogg (1970) has written extensively about the art of children and the universality of certain basic shapes. Her study of many thousands of drawings, paintings, and clayworks of preschool children allowed her to make rigorous comparisons of the shapes they use with those found in prehistoric and primitive arts. She also touches on some psychological and aesthetic theories of symbolism. I will restrict what follows to my own experience.

Babies first make images of their gestures by scratching or smearing surfaces with their fingers or thrusting their heels in sand or mud. A seated child creates direction lines outward from his body with his feet, but a pen or pencil held in the hand tends to be used laterally at first. Later, he pushes the line away and, as he becomes practised, this continuous scribble contains eliptical shapes or single lines that have been broken off and restarted elsewhere (Figure 3.2a). A particular spot in the pictorial area may be favoured by continuous scribbling until it becomes quite dark, and single, thrusting lines tend to start from this position (Figure 3.2b). These 'centredness markings' (Kellogg 1970) seem to act as a focal point for the extended movements, to which they return. I watched one baby of fourteen months scribbling, then, starting from a central point near to his body, he pushed the marker up the page. He showed excitement when the marker went over the edge of the drawing pad and repeated this several times. His pleasure then seemed to change from sensation of the marker bumping over the edge of the pad to a new satisfaction in stopping the line just before it got to the edge.

When circles begin to hold a child's attention, he tends to draw over any that he sees in his scribble and later to draw them outside the scribble on a blank space (Figure 3.2c). However, empty circles seem to become unsatisfactory to the child for often the centre is filled with scribbling, or circles, lines, or dots (Figure 3.2e). Some other primates respond creatively to empty squares (Morris 1962: 60). Lines may be thrust through the boundary of the circle giving an effect of movement or force. Often the shape of a square is made from a continuous line or several separate strokes, which may be straight or curved following the edge of the drawing paper (Figure 3.2g). Then it is clear that the motor pleasure described by Kellogg and others has given way to the satisfaction of creating a particular shape. Neither the circle nor the square are easy to make, yet we see toddlers deliberately jerking their way round with a line until its end reaches its beginning again.

The importance of a closed circle can be seen in drawings where the point of closure is worked over as though a knot was being tied (Figure 3.2b). Such deliberate and laborious acts are quite different from the random scribbles that children make at other times. Precision is needed to return the drawing point to a particular place if the shape or density does not satisfy the child. At about the same time that circles are created we see a square framing a circle (Figure 3.2c) When these shapes are drawn on a blank surface it seems as if they are experienced as boundary lines; however, when they have been completed, the circular or square area that is

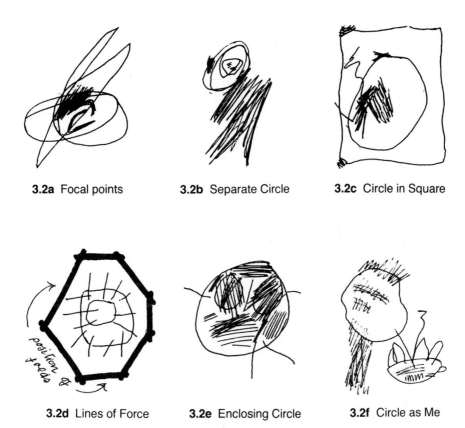

3.2a Focal points   **3.2b** Separate Circle   **3.2c** Circle in Square

3.2d Lines of Force   **3.2e** Enclosing Circle   **3.2f** Circle as Me

3.2g Attributes of Me   **3.2h** Square as Me   **3.2i** Circle as House

Figure 3.2 Diagram. The development of symbolic images

enclosed becomes more important than the outline, and is often used as a space to put things in.

Lines crossing the circle or radiating from it become important parts of a drawing, made with deliberate effect as lines of force. A child may stop a line at a certain place by drawing another at right angles to it or box it inside a circle or a square. These abstract shapes may be decorated with dots, lines, small circles and so on that come in time to identify the shape; and then it may be given a name. In the next stage these simple, geometric marks are arranged in ways that allow the onlooker to recognize them as attributes of a particular object – a face, a house and so on. By the end of latency a child can portray anything he wishes from this assembly kit of simple shapes.

During the course of this development, if children have access to paints, they enjoy making bright masses of colour. Scribbled lines are fused by the wider strokes of a brush. This develops into overworking, such as we saw in the focal points of early linear scribbles, but now spontaneous explorations with colours tends to lead to overpainting, an original area of colour being altered, sometimes time and again; often, this seems to happen when a colour does not seem bright enough in contrast to the surrounding colours.

Before we look for further meaning in this form of art it is useful to compare its changing appearance with other styles associated with Archaic art. A child's first scribbles are quite similar to the Linear Transition. Some of these show closed shapes and focal points while others have a chaotic effect that is typical of that part of the Linear Transition that I describe as its particular style. In the next stage a child deliberately uses shapes based on circles and squares to show objects that can be recognized by their attributes – trees, houses, people and so on. When several images occupy one area their scale is diminished and, as more attributes are included, the symmetry of the work becomes upset and geometric shapes give way to the irregularities caused, for instance, by profile views, or overlapping. The shapes eventually become more or less approximations of visible appearances. If such representations dominate a drawing or painting, we find that Archaic art has given way to the Traditional naturalism of the Western world.

Naming or entitling arises, I suppose, when a child can share some of his experiences in speech. In our eagerness to understand what a child is drawing we may encourage naming by asking questions about his work. But the child, who is an Archaic artist, does not represent the outer world in his work, even if he is led to describe it in these terms. The three-year-old who painted Figure 3.1, and ran about with it saying that she had painted buns for everyone, found what she wanted to paint after it was done. Her title described what the picture finally looked and felt like to her, although the circular masses might be interpreted by an adult as 'really' giving her mother or father a lot of babies or faeces! However, the meaning of an abstract painting remains symbolic, that is to say that it has the qualities that Freud describes as belonging to the primary process, the archaic heritage that a child brings with him into the world. This, he says, is 'an inclination to form fresh unities out of elements which in our waking thoughts we should certainly keep separate' (Freud 1949a: 28–9). In fact, the meaning that a young child gives to his picture can change from day to day, even from minute to minute because he sees it as a mirror that extends his conscious understanding.

There is a danger that we may pay too much attention to the subject matter and neglect the importance of the creative process itself: if we do this a drawing or painting comes to be used like a home-made Rorschach and Thematic Apperception Test. Although a child may be reminded of something by the look of his painting and name it accordingly, this name may bear no relation to the original impulse that created the work. In this case we might tentatively consider that the little girl who painted the 'buns' showed at that moment, in her general feeling for their arrangement round the circle, a need to give places to a number of things and also the pleasure of sharing.

THE BIRTH OF SYMBOLIC IMAGERY

Speech must be learnt but symbolic images are innate, born anew with every child. They are an Archaic heritage (Freud 1949a: 28). Winnicott describes the birth of the individual, or unit self.

> In the beginning the infant is the environment and the environment is the infant. By a complex process (which is in part understood and on which I and others have written at great length) the infant separates out objects and the environment from the self.   (Winnicott 1986: 72)

In a section concerning the localization of the mind, he says (my italics):

> An *inner* world of personal imaginative experience therefore comes into the scheme of things and shared reality is on the whole thought of as *outside* the personality. Although babies cannot draw pictures, I think they are capable (except through lack of skill) of depicting themselves by a circle at certain moments in their first months ... using the circle or sphere as a diagram of the self.   (Winnicott 1978: 253)

From this Winnicott concludes that:

> one of the many consequences of this development is that the infant comes to have an Inside. A complex interchange between what is inside now begins and continues throughout the individual's life and constitutes the main relationship of the individual to the world. (Winnicott 1986: 72)

As I see it, this complex interchange is symbolized by the circle in the square. The outer periphery of the circle is at the same time the inner boundary of the area of the square. The spontaneous appearance of this arrangement is vital at times when only a visual image can give shape to otherwise intolerable confusion arising from a failure to place an experience either inside or outside the self.

> It is easy to observe that children draw or paint geometrical pictures corresponding to those described by Jung as symbols of the self. These are figures, usually circular in shape, having a centre and a varying internal structure.   (Fordham 1976: 15)

It is possible that the circles and lines that seem to be symbolic could be first created by the shape or function of the eye before consciousness distinguishes perceptions from the perceiving ego. These dissociated perceptions might also account for light patterns discernible with closed eyes (Kellogg, Knoll and Kugler 1968). Lack of eye movement, as in staring, might be projected as a circle of focused vision, or, when unfocused, become the basis of introspections, and daydreams in which one sees oneself in the mind's eye. On the other hand, mobile eye movements used in following and separating out the individual parts of a scene might be interpreted as directional lines (Matthews 1984), which I term 'lines of force'. In short, the symbolic shapes of Self and Other may originate kinaesthetically. Although it may be difficult for adults to imagine babies abstracting these shapes from the visible world when they begin to draw and paint we do see that they are sensitive to the space that is available and make their drawings relate to it. For example, if the child draws on a small piece of writing paper, the circle tends to expand to its limits, rather as we might stretch out in a cramped position; but if the space is very large, such as a steamy windowpane, the child often draws a square round his circle to enclose it (3.2d). A girl of four and a half, when first taken into care, drew a very large square round the edge of the drawing paper, then, using dots, she made a tiny circle in the middle of this empty space.

We generally approach a work of art first through its subject matter and then respond subconsciously to the effect of its style. There is little variety in the subject matter of young children's art and we often pass over the symbolic implications of the style – the placement, proportions and so on. Consequently, the force of the communication is lost. We can appreciate the extent to which an artist, adult or child, thinks with his hands and eyes when we respond to the symbolism of the basic shapes of the circle as a self-image and the square as the image of all that is not self. The child's drawing of a circle with lines of force (Figure 3.2f) can be seen as 'my self doing something'. Read simply in this way we are not bothered by the fact that the image has no body or arms (Freeman 1975). After all, we would not expect the child to describe first each of his limbs when he only wanted to tell us something about his legs.

The circle of self may have the attributes of the sun or a flower: this symbolically expresses a subjective experience – me, the flower, me, the sun. When an adult paints a flower or the sun, he may wish to be objective about the sun or the flower.

When we consider the square as a symbolic image, it is the boundary of all that is not experienced as not the self, a place where the self can, or cannot be (Figure 3.4). In their uses of the square it looks as if there is something wrong in the child's life if the circle cannot be used as the self, or the square as the other; for example, when a circle is contained or bounded by another circle (Figure 3.6), or when the attributes of a house are given to the circle (Figure 3.2i). A square head or body seems particularly poignant, indicating that part which seems alien and other than self (Figure 3.2h). Of course, in all this the basic distinction between a temporary mood and an habitual attitude must be considered.

When the basic symbolism of circles and squares is extended by attributes, these are first rendered in circles and squares that are not only symbolic but also signify definite, whole objects such as eyes, noses and so on. Figure 3.2g shows both sorts of image in one drawing. The symbolic image of the self has attributes of a face, while only three of the four symbolic lines of force are given the attributes of limbs. A two and a half-year-old boy called his drawing (Figure 3.2f) *Me a big boy with dog,* but the title alone does not help us to understand why he draws himself without arms, legs or body. However, if we see the circle as self with lines of force, we can realize that the child does not present himself as an object in the way that he has drawn the dog with the attributes of legs; this makes the subjective view of himself understandable. He cannot see himself as he can see the dog.

During the years in which a child spontaneously expresses himself as an Archaic artist, he uses an integrated visual language that imposes the subjective view of circles and squares upon everything he paints and draws. This vision allows him to reach out into the complexities of the external world from within a circle of self that is firmly held within the finite boundary of the square. Within the limits of these basic shapes he can draw anything that comes into his head, adding more and more details from his developing experience until the day comes when he sees, or is shown, that the world has a surface appearance and that he also can be seen from the other side of the looking-glass. This is a moment of truth in which modern life gives no help, for it has no means to express in everyday language that inner world in which we also live. Then the child sees that when art has an appearance of shared reality it is preferred, and Archaic imagery is degraded as childish or primitive. At puberty most children give up creative initiative and try to live as if they were only related to the outer world. Adolescence can be a desperate time if the split between inner and outer life seems to be without any means of integration at all. Before this, children between the ages of nine and eleven often divide their art styles according to the subject matter. A subject that refers to the inner world, such as a king or a house being made as an Archaic image while those referring to perceptions or ideas tend to be presented in a Traditional style. This flexibility seems general in latency. In a study (Simon 1976) only one child in a group of eighty used the same style for a king, a house, a landscape and an interior.

SYMBOLIC INTEGRATIONS IN CHILD ART

It seems that symbolic images of integration are continually discovered by young children and shaped with sand or mud or painted and drawn. They often need a square of the right size or shape to contain the circle. For instance, the hexagon in Figure 3.2d was made by folding back the surplus area of the square. Although we rarely talk about symbolic images to children they often show that they understand the symbolism of their art (Fordham 1976). The solid, energetic little girl who painted *Buns for everyone* (Figure 3.1) enjoyed nursery school and the many activities that were offered. When she painted the square of magenta circles she placed one in the centre which was about the same size as the others. It had plenty of space around it in which it could have been enlarged; however, it seemed that she had found the circle of self to be proportionate to those of others. As I see it, this image of integration is a very impressive achievement for a young child; perhaps she felt this too, for she wanted her picture off the easel straight away so that she could take it round to show that she had made buns for everyone.

Clarice was a different type of child, a serious little girl who had found some difficulty in coping with nursery school. At first she could not play with other children but spent all her time at the easel, painting with her back to the room. At first she painted a stereotyped image of a house facade, such as one might expect from a child of five or six. Over the following weeks this house became taller and much thinner (Figure 3.3a), then she gave it up altogether and made a series of abstract patterns based on circles and squares (Figures 3.3b, e and f). After this abstract phase she made complex arrangements of the basic symbols which were sometimes named, such as *Lady knitting* (Figure 3.3g). Then these developed attributes that were organized to create recognizable images (Figure 3.3h). The final drawing in this series (Figure 3.3j) shows a figure that refers to something beyond itself; part of the square is painted blue and has the attribute of a sky. The nursery school teacher felt that this child had used painting as a sort of self-therapy. Once she had shed an inappropriate drawing skill and become more relaxed; she began to use the toys and play with the other children.

As life presents new experiences we need to create new means of

3.3a   **3.3b**   **3.3c**   **3.3d**

3.3e   **3.3f**   **3.3g**

3.3h   **3.3i**   **3.3j**

Paintings by Clarice, a three-year-old made during her first six months in nursery school showing the developmental sequence indicated in Figure 3.2, including a therapeutic regression from Figure 3.3a.

a. Self Circle as a window – black roof in stereotyped house Square.
b. Self Circle solid infilling inside Squares.
c. Separate Circle-in-Square motifs.
d. Attachment/separation symbol (see also Figure 3.7).
e. Attachment/separation: Circles outside Square.
f.   Self Circle: solid, included with other small Circles and Squares.
g. Self Circle with impacted Lines of Force. Attributes of 'Lady Knitting'.
h. Self Circle with infilled body attributes. Self Circle as sun with Lines of Force.
i.   Self Circle with attributes of a cat.
j.   Self Circle with attributes. Representation of sky – boundless shape.

Figure 3.3 Diagram of Clarice's pictures

integrating them with our sense of self. Symbolic images reflect the quality of these integrations in a particular style. An example of this need to integrate the basic image of the circle to a changing pattern in a normal family can be seen in the painting made by a six-year-old girl during a holiday art group session (Figure 3.4). A narrow dark house is placed in the centre of a wide piece of paper. The attributes of the house itself are muddled and messy but one can see the garden, its people, a dog and some plants. The only colours used are blue and black with yellow for the sun, the chimney, the smoke and some details of the figures. When the painting was finished it was time to go home, but the girl kept her mother waiting while she hunted for a pencil. With this she drew circles with radiating lines above each figure, including the dog, saying 'Everybody must have their own spider's web'. I hope that the reader can see for himself that, whatever else can be surmised from the content of the picture, the basic symbolic images of Circles were chosen to present something important, separate and distinct from the dark, muddly house.

Figure 3.2 is not offered as an invariable progression but to indicate the main stages usually taken from simple to complex forms, of children's art. These stages may coexist for various lengths of time and any one might be omitted or continued as an habitual attitude into adult life as, for instance the scribbles of 'motor pleasure' are used in the art of tachism. Although

Figure 3.4 *'Everybody must have their own spider's web'* Massive Transition

my purpose in this work is to study the therapeutic effects of creating art I do not want to imply that this must be confined entirely to a special therapeutic setting. As the nursery school teacher said, children such as Clarice do themselves a therapy and most bumps, cuts and scratches self-heal. Even some bad cuts, wounds and infections heal from within, although there are some sorts of damage that need outside help and others that cannot be repaired at all. The examples that follow indicate self-healing through creative activities that needed the special setting of thera-peutic sessions and the attention of the therapist; they do not provide a generally applicable technique, unless it be in the minimal use of inter-vention. They are given as a means of bringing to life the theoretical material and to show the reader something of the setting in which my ideas came to light.

Jennie was a rather withdrawn and docile girl of ten who had been coming weekly from a residential home for art as therapy. When we began to discuss the holiday break to come she had just completed a delicate charcoal and coloured drawing and was standing beside it, ready to leave at the end of the session. The drawing was of a young teenager, surrounded by the things Jennie considered adult – high-heeled shoes, glass of wine and reclining chair. As I reminded her of the coming holiday she took a brush full of black paint and idly encircled the face in her picture, going round and round until the heavy outline transformed its appearance to that of a young child. Then she overpainted the whole figure, including the features of the face, to which she added black tears or freckles. Taking a light green pastel, she added a bubble from the mouth and faint words, *'Stay here'.* The words make explicit the symbolic meaning of the heavy *circle* of the self (Figure 3.5).

The following example examines a context in which the integrating symbols of circle and square appeared intermittently, as focal points in the content of frantic play. When circles and squares arose spontaneously they had twofold value, reflecting the essence of the child's problem to himself and also to me. Although I did not interpret these symbolic images to him, or even remark on the need for them, they did create a rapport between us. As they signalled the progress of the therapeutic work that was occurring I could go along with his need for chaotic play, which seemed like the scribbling, motor pleasure of a baby's first drawing and painting. The circles and squares, appearing in manifold ways were like marker buoys above a submerged object. Over two and a half years of therapy this child redis-covered his whole self, inside and outside, in relation to various difficult or traumatic experiences. I have also used this case to show the sort of occasion when I might alter my usual approach and offer a suggestion when a patient seems stuck in a routine or ritual. In this case I managed to do this at the right moment and the patient used my suggestion to make a thera-peutic leap forward.

Figure 3.5 'Stay here' Traditional to Archaic

Pippi was five and a half when he started therapy. His mother told me that she was depressed at the time of his birth and for the following year but his father successfully 'mothered' the baby. He had seemed a sleepy baby and rather slow to sit and stand. When he was two, Pippi was found to be deaf and, although surgical treatment was successful, his mother felt that it had been a terrible shock, 'because of the noise'. He changed from a contented baby to a restless, intractable child. When Pippi entered primary education his teacher felt unable to understand him: he was well above average in reading and spelling but would not write properly, or draw, or attend in any group work. He needed constant attention and his teacher recommended special education. However, his devoted parents managed to persuade the school to keep him on.

At his first visit Pippi launched himself into my house and had to be restrained from running all over it. He was small, thin, fair and big-boned with an awkwardness of movement that was so marked that I felt myself expecting him to fall over although he eventually kept his balance by lurching and stumbling along. He frequently protruded his tongue when he spoke and this made him difficult to understand; however, I noticed that he could call clearly from a distance. His voice was loud and harsh as if he still had difficulty in hearing himself speak.

The first session was chaotic. As my studio had been damaged in a recent storm we used the kitchen in my house and he raced about, handling everything and talking non-stop at the top of his voice. I did hear two references to fire – fire in the chip pan and a Christmas tree that had accidently caught alight. Otherwise, this session seemed fully taken up by my efforts to contain him in one room. The second and subsequent sessions were held in the studio. This space seemed less frightening, and Pippi was less distracted. He took a piece of paper, $12 \times 10\frac{1}{2}$ inches and painted a red, diagonally placed 'I' which he ringed with dots of green paint, themselves encircled with dots of red (Figure 3.6). He explained that he had drawn a capital I surrounded by red and green fairies. I was pleased to have a painting and a story to go with it and offered to write down the story for him. He directed me to write on the side of the painting and dictated:

> *'The Big I'* had lovely circles round it, they were there to protect and catch any fire that was there, burning away at the Big I. The greens are big cranes that lift the Big I and put it somewhere neat and tidy so that the fire can't get at it. The red circle of flames are getting rather near the Big I.

Pippi put this painting aside and asked for some clay but could not bear to touch it. He asked me to hold it while he made a weak attempt to bang it with a mallet. His balance was so poor that, in his efforts to swing the wooden mallet he toppled over. He asked me what such a wooden hammer was called and when I said it was a mallet he said that 'Hammer' was like

Figure 3.6 'The Big I' Archaic Linear

his name. He asked the name of the measuring instrument for clay work and, being told that they were called callipers, he set them up on a block of clay and said, 'This is a handicap.' Pointing to the marks made by the mallet on the clay, he suddenly became tyrannical. 'You! Wipe your hands on your trousers as I do. They're dirty. This is a house, these are windows ... can't you see them?' When I said 'I see' he was disconcerted and touched my hand, saying 'It's only in fun.'

In the third session he found the wire claycutters and cut up quantities of clay. As he could not bear to touch the clay I had to hold the bolts upright while he looped the wire over them and sliced them up. If I tried to say anything he feigned deafness, shouting 'What, what, what?' He hit the clay with the mallet and succeeded in hitting me quite hard with it, although I tried to avoid it. Using a piece of wood, he levered a block of clay over the edge of the table on to the floor; he sponged the top surface of it with water and stuck some paper on it. At first he seemed to pretend that he was wiping or bandaging the damage caused by the fall, but he then developed the idea of making a picture from the wet clay marks on the paper and eventually completed seventeen clay prints that were laid out all over the floor of the studio. He described these as pictures and told me what they represented but I could not see any representations in them. In one instance he said:

> This is a house, it is superb. It's a hut, nobody is in it, it's full of clay and paint and things to play with. This is my garden, my apple tree, one half brown and one half green. The chickens can fly when they are five.

Pippi's actual use of the art materials was minimal: they were only props for his stories. He used paper, paint rags and water or small stones and twigs brought into the studio. For several months after '*The Big I*' painting he did not make anything at all or fix an image and it was often as difficult to keep up with his fantasies as it was to contain his activities within the bounds of safety. Some themes recurred, such as, fire dangers, and pairs of things. To image the latter he used two mallets, the handles of the clay cutters that were attached to each other with wire in acting out stories of aeroplanes tied together. He did not want these stories written. Two objects fought – the big mallet and the smaller one hit each other relentlessly. Pippi impressed on me that only strong people could play these games and made me stand well back. He often hurt himself or fell during these fights but was brave and did not cry. Sometimes he told me to hold one end of a piece of string while he held the other. There was no tug-of-war in this; he assumed the authority to choose who would let go of the string. However, the power of choice seemed to make him uneasy: often he managed to let his end slip away, as if by accident, and in that way the game would come to an end.

Eventually he began to paint again, first making two overlapping circles with thick, overlapping strokes, and then a single circle, nine inches in diameter, using short, heavy strokes overpainted several times with mauve paint on black paper. He was excited by this creation, and said:

> This is a beautiful colour. I love painting. This is an island. It is my head I think. I think it is my brain and there is my hair at the side. It's a beautiful morning; the sun shines down beautifully.... I am standing on the grass in a beautiful evening sunset.

Pippi seemed really enraptured by this large, complete circle but did not attempt to add the colours of the beautiful morning and the sunset: the actual colours were black paper and purple paint. After this he began to make some things in clay – hills and roads and, later, planes and cars that were given a few attributes and allowed to present a single image rather than a string of discrete associations. During the sessions preceding the summer break Pippi made his first pot, a circular, heavy object about six inches in diameter. Inside was a solid ring of clay attached to the sides of the pot by four clay walls or spokes. On the outside he spread pieces of clay, giving an effect of two faces. (Another child had made a pot with faces painted on the outside, and Pippi may have seen this.) Pippi said:

> This pot has two faces and it is a fruit one. One face has spectacles and that is the back one, the front one just has eyes. The nose and mouth got wiped off. The front one is like Pippi and the back one is Mrs Simon.

Pippi's use of 'found objects' had led to regular play with a feather duster on a long handle that he needed regularly to brush my studio walls in case of spiders. This play had a compulsive feel to it, and after some time I began to feel that we might have had enough of it. Certainly, I felt it had outrun its symbolic usefulness.

The holiday time had been very successful. His mother was much happier about him, his tongue no longer protruded, he looked stronger and a bit fatter, he was clear of ear infections and was learning to swim. His speech was clear, though still pretty loud and he now enjoyed balancing on a chair, which he could tilt on my uneven studio floor, rocking on this and testing his balance as he talked, or worked with the clay. He was learning to ride his brother's bike, in spite of falls and grazes. His interest in pairs of things continued. He talked about twins and boys who had the same first name. Fighting continued between two lumps of clay and he became interested in magic. The waste water bucket would be draped with rags or papers for some marvellous experiment or conjuring trick. I had to close my eyes while preparations were made. In these games I felt that Pippi was marking time to cope with increasing pressures outside, the extra tuition, swimming lessons and an unaccompanied air flight with a younger sibling to another country for a few days' holiday.

It is usual in work with children to find that improvement in their be-haviour outside the session is seen as time to withdraw the child from therapy. Understandably, once symptoms have been relieved, parents want their child to return to the ordinary rough and tumble of everyday life; but I felt that Pippi was not yet ready for this. His worries about spiders' webs seemed to symbolize a problem that needed to be given a more potent image than the theatrical prop that was provided by his discovery of my feather duster. Although I do not often need to plan a session, and much prefer to follow than lead, I felt that Pippi might now be invited to paint the webs he feared to find, instead of trying to get rid of them magically, before they could appear. When I suggested this, he seemed to like the idea of showing me the webs in a picture, and took a sheet of blue paper on which he painted an orange circle about the size of a teacup on the left-hand side. He said, 'Here is a web. I'll show you how to paint it: you paint it like a splodge.' At that moment he took blue paint into his brush and scribbled in the top right-hand corner of the paper with the mixture of blue and orange that made a muddy brown. This colour he used to fill and almost cover the orange circle, and then he drew a diagonal line linking the two masses of paint (Figure 3.7). Pippi suddenly looked very anxious and turned the painting round, so that the position of the splodges was reversed. The spider's web was now in place of the covered orange circle. He sounded quite frightened. 'Here is a *big* circle. It is a green spider with red eyes. The fire came and burnt its eyes and its legs.' Pippi hurriedly put the painting aside and took a sheet of orange paper and some pale mauve paint, making a squarish circle. He said, 'Now we must have more paper. The circle is me, purple, my best colour. Orange is for my hair. The cup handles are ears; you make one one way and the other the other way.' This circle is made with two strokes (Figure 3.8), the diameter is exactly nine inches, including the hair. This was the first face that Pippi had painted, although he had already modelled features on the clay pot some weeks before. His large, sweeping movements, and the coordinated features of this first-ever portrait painting strongly suggested that Pippi was at that movement very much at home in his body and its gestural expressiveness.

At the top of this painting he made a criss-cross of lines in black and I asked if it was the spider. Pippi said it was a crossroads. He then went back to the spider's web painting and used thick white paint to work over the line of the broomstick. He asked me to draw arrows to show what things were; at the top I was to write 'This is a broom.' Below this I had to put 'This is me, one eye is blurred, the mouth is all spotty like teeth. The mouth is open and talking. The white is the good Pippi cleaning ALL the bad cobwebs.' After this session Pippi did not use the feather duster again.

The third session I wish to describe took place a year later and by this time Pippi was fitting into normal life at home and school, being considered by his mother to be a clever little monkey who needed pushing. On this occasion he gave the impression of coming for a particular purpose, running through the door shouting 'What? What? What?' as he had done

Figure 3.7 *Broom and splodge* Archaic Transition

Figure 3.8 *Good Pippi* Archaic Linear

in the old days when he had taken refuge in deafness. He was now nearly seven.

He immediately set to work with the clay, making a solid cube by banging a large piece on the table. He cut this into four, saying 'This must be cut in pieces: these three must be put over there [on another table]. They are the children and they don't belong here.' Then he rolled out a coil of clay and brought the ends together to form a circle which was immediately filled by a mass of clay to make a round pile about five inches high. The base of the mass was then scooped out at one side and he said, 'I have made a fortress. It's very tall, it has a big mouth and inside is a "rover". This is a dungeon – we will scoop it out.' Pippi was too excited to do this properly. The 'rover' block of clay was too large to fit into the hole he had made at the base of the fortress and it projected from the side. He said, 'I will make two wheels. Please will you roll up clay balls for the wheels. [I did.] These will go on top of the fortress. The car is really a bridge – I will make it tall for the tall ships and the small ships to go in, but the castle flies about and rocks in the wind and crashes down and squashes the bridge and the man was walking about on the bridge and he was knocked into the sea.'

Pippi laughed wildly as he bashed the fortress. He added, 'And the balls on top.' Then he snatched them off. Pippi continued, 'And the balls are one ball rolled into the dungeon and it was cracked open.'

Pippi tried to roll the two balls into one but he was too excited to do this smoothly and the single ball he made showed the join. He did not actually put the ball into the ruined dungeon, which was still stuffed with the clay block called the Rover or bridge. Then Pippi became quite quiet and looked terribly unhappy and crushed. For my own sake I felt that I must come in to the play for a moment. I asked, 'When it cracked open, what was inside?' Pippi said:

> It was a baby, and they opened it up and found inside the baby with its eyes full of blood and they took care of it. Can you please make the baby's head? It wants to hold its blankie and its all rolled up. It's six years old, let's pretend.

I said we might make some arms for the baby to hold its rolled up blankie and Pippi became calmer, interested in the clay ball. He said it had to have ears to hear its Mummy and Daddy. The play was resumed in a semi-shared way. Pippi took the coils of clay I made and wrapped them round the ball and I scratched with my fingernail to make a face. Then suddenly Pippi became excited again. He took the clay block from the ruined fortress to use as a bed for the baby, saying 'Its Daddy and Mummy love it and take it to bed and he loves his Mummy but not his Daddy; his Daddy is jealous and so he doesn't like him but he loves his Mummy because he came out of her.'

Pippi put the baby on the 'Rover', saying, 'This will be a boat. I must have six pieces of paper. They must be dried so they can keep off all the cobwebs.' He shouted, 'I *must* have a motorboat to go on the water. Please, can we pretend that he is six and his arms are oars in the water and it goes round the arms and the islands like this.' He picked up the 'roverboat' and showed how it went through the water, steering well away from the broken fortress. This play did not depend upon words alone but he showed me just where the boat would go. When the session ended, Pippi reduced his demand for paper to two sheets which I gave him to take home.

Pippi's parents loved him dearly and had great expectations of him, based upon his evident intelligence. However, he had been born with a real disability that had not been diagnosed before he was two years old. In spite of successful operations to his ears it seemed to him that he had not been made well and was handicapped like children he may have seen in hospital, who cannot walk without callipers. When he set up the modelling tool in a lump of clay he formed an image for this assumption, and having given his fear a shape could challenge it. Later he frequently tested his balance on the high stool on my uneven floor and then further by learning to swim and ride a bicycle.

Then he was able to move naturally. I do not mean that Pippi's weird gait had been assumed deliberately but that the sight of handicapped children who were trying to walk provided an image of his anxious tension when he was hospitalized during the ages of two and four. The ear operations might temporarily have disturbed the sense of balance which he had as a toddler, so recently acquired. This is perhaps to suggest that he introjected, in the psychoanalytic sense, rather than identified with, or copied a lame child. In some other cases I have seen similar effects of an introjection that belongs to an early period before there has been a split between inner and outer reality. Put another way, the child has not achieved a complete circle: part of it was made up by the area of the square. Without the ability to find a complete circle of self Pippi had been prey to any experience that might be used to give meaning to his sense of fragmentation. He seems to have taken in the sight of a handicapped child's distended tongue and also preserved his own past experience of deafness and lack of speech; even the temporary incontinence could have been another means of imaging his unthinkable sense of physical disability. His parents' continuing belief in his superior intelligence could do no more in this muddle than give him a sense of being only an ego – a big I, that was in great danger from his burning fire of dissociated rage. At school even the special talents of this big I were found wanting, for he could not relate to other children or play in team games. He could only learn when he had the teacher's undivided attention. It seemed to Pippi that he was not fully fledged to meet his first school year – like chickens that can fly when they are five.

PIPPI'S VERBAL THINKING

I had been told that Pippi had a reading age of eight but could not draw or paint and would not learn to write, in spite of early home tuition. It seemed that his speech had recently deteriorated, due to his loud, garbled production and also the tongue projections. However, this improved when he needed to tell me the stories that he visualized round paint and clay, but could not actually materialize in paint or clay. He would not let me write down these early fantasies for him, perhaps because this would have slowed him down. Other children who use a flight of ideas without pausing to create images may seem to deafen and confuse themselves and me unless they can use my help in writing down their stories and poems. During the early times when Pippi was using words as if they were almost dissociated from thoughts I was met by hubbub and hyperactivity. However, in time his aptitude for words became linked with play and he could be very poetic, as in the story of the hut that arose from his first painting of a circle.

THE CIRCLES AND SQUARES

The day that Pippi made that first circle could be said to be a 'birth day'. I do not think that the delight he expressed in his story was excessive or the equation of the hut/head/brain/beautiful sunrise and sunset an inappropriate expression of his joy in finding an image of himself as whole and beautiful in a beautiful world. I think that at that moment he began to be well. His previous play had been concerned with the broken or fragmented circle, worries about splitting – children who were different but had the same name, the battle between two similar mallets, and so on. He had fought these battles for identity very bravely but hopelessly. First one and then the other would win, then the first winner would score again, endlessly symbolizing the split between his inner and outer needs and the growing threat of what Winnicott would call a false self, dissociated from his inner life. His fingers were often hurt in the process, his toes and his poor knees banged on my cement floor, but as he stared at his sore limbs in dismay he would not cry. He had done the hurt to himself.

The fruit bowl that Pippi made just before the summer holidays is an interesting symbol of his integrative impulse at that time. He first made a heavy circle which had a base, forming the attribute of an inside. On this base he built another circle – like the keep inside a castle – and seemed to anchor it with the spoke-like strips of clay, or lines of force that, nevertheless remained inside the larger sphere. On the outside of the bowl he roughly spread clay to represent his features and mine also, as if he needed an outer self, together with my self, to contain his inner self and the food it could hold. His act in wiping off the mouth on the outside of the pot might have been another aspect of his determination not to cry.

I return now to the extraordinary painting of the cobweb and the broom. Pippi seemed quite interested in the idea of painting the cobwebs because they did not go away when he wiped them with his feather duster. He started with a smallish orange circle which, I think, symbolized himself or his hand, or the broom perhaps. Then came the shapeless splodge that seemed to be too frightening to remain at the top of the page and was brought down by the device of turning the paper round. However, this put the circle at the top and the circle now looked very big to him, a green spider with red eyes, while, I imagine, Pippi was now imaged as the shapeless splodge. In defence against this disintegrated mass Pippi took fresh paper and made his first image of a face, a self-portrait of the good Pippi and, having made it, he returned to the frightening picture of the disintegrated Pippi and gave me a description of the whole horror – the blurred eye, the spotty mouthful of teeth that are talking. With white paint he drew the line of force, as an act of wiping away the cobwebs of fear and revenge that he had projected on to the walls of my studio. Then, by turning the paper round Pippi had shown himself that the cobweb was not out there, but in himself and in those few moments had withdrawn a projection that could have taken months of verbal psychotherapy to withdraw.

Pippi used the symbols of circle and square in the session of clay work in which the square, as an image of the outer world, was formed as a block and then sliced into four 'children'. Three of these were put aside and the fourth was called a 'Rover', thrust into the base of the fortress and then transformed into a bridge and a boat. In these transformations he played out his conflicts about bridging and breaking, destroying and creating. In the stage of destruction, the car wheels were put safely on top of the fortress, but his failure to make a single sphere (as an image of the circle of self) seems to have made him despair. The crack in the egg appeared to reflect his fear of being split apart, cracked and mad. However, he could use my intervention to image the self as a loved baby but, to my surprise this led him straight on to the idea of jealousy and the Oedipal situation.

Pippi used the block of clay as a motorboat that needed oars for its propulsion. I felt that this expressed a need for initiatives – to be self-propelled. The six pieces of paper that were so urgently desired could be seen as his way of showing that he felt the need for a lifetime to recover himself. However, in fact before he left the session he had modified this demand to a couple of sheets, or years. In fact Pippi's therapy was contained in thirty-six sessions, spread over two and a half years. Then I considered him to be well enough to leave, on the understanding that he could return if he needed to. He continued to cope well at school and with the high standards of his family, taking the examinations needed for secondary education at the usual time. His last months of therapy were not dramatic: he spent most of it in playing out his need to take care of himself and be his own man. He hid things and found them again, he filled clothes' lines with dripping 'nappies' created with paint-rags and drew an image of himself as a whole figure, a punk caveman who is not a respectable caveman for one of his toe-hairs got burnt when he wasn't looking.

In summary this chapter presents the idea of a basic symbolic image of a circle innate, an archaic heritage arising spontaneously in every child in response to the need for self-definition. The symbolic circle in the square affirms our wholeness and our integration of the split between the reality inside and outside. I have given Pippi's story in special detail, in order to show the way symbolic images are embedded in the style and content of art as therapy.

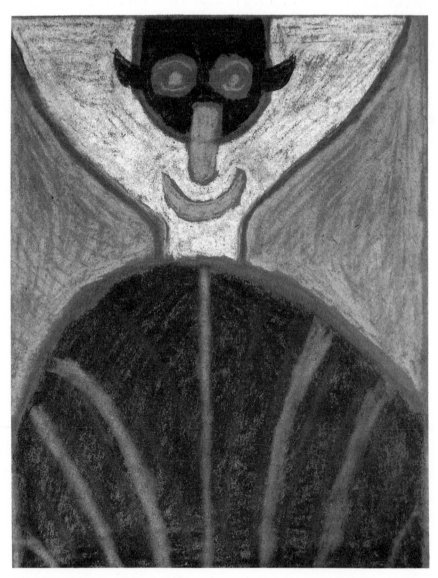

Figure 4.1 *'Moses'* Archaic Linear

Chapter 4

The Archaic Linear style
Images of sensuous life

In Chapter 1 I introduced a theory of art styles; four basic styles linked by four transitional areas, each with its particular character. These form a complete circle which encompasses Traditional and Archaic art. In Chapter 3 I outlined the stages of child art which follow the same order of styles in a clockwise direction. The art styles of young children are considered to be living examples of Archaic art and the symbolic imagery of these early works reflects a basic need for an integrative image to contain our conflicting experiences of inner and outer reality. The primary image of integration is seen in the vital relation of the circle to the square. This symbolic imagery underlies more complex forms of adult art and in this chapter I will trace its appearance and meaning in the Archaic Linear style. My particular concern here is with its place in therapeutic work with deeply disturbed people who may have been ill in one way and another for a very long time.

THE APPEARANCE

Archaic art is still found in some primitive cultures and also in the work of professional artists exhibiting alongside the more Traditional styles. Artists such as Picasso have extended a large area of the culture of our times to make room for those painters or sculptors who are dominated by their awareness of the sensuous quality of art. Other artists may consciously adopt some form of primitivism as an escape from the bondage of a perceptual art form. Only their freedom from affectation will allow them to escape the limitations of one stereotype for the other.

Although some works in this style are not large, all give an impression of huge scale through the simplicity and geometry of the shapes which are clearly outlined. The effect is strange, formal and unrealistic (Figure 4.1). Clear outlines are not obscured by any colour/tones within them and the regular outlines flatten shapes even when tones are varied in an attempt to give an effect of form. The two-dimensionality emphasizes the proportional relation between shapes that are based on circles and squares.

POSTURE AND GESTURE

Many of these artists almost dance before their canvasses, or caress their sculptures, responding to the art material with effortless grace that involves their whole body in the creative act. Their vision is wide and relatively unfocused and this psychophysical openness is reflected in the large scale of the work. The artist can draw a perfect circle with one continuous movement because he can see in his mind's eye both before and behind the movement of his hand; similarly his brush can trace a perfectly straight line as if it was propelled by gravity or traversing some preordained path. There is no place for will in this art: will tenses the muscles in its effort to achieve its aim. Psychophysical coordination demands emotional detachment and a diminution of the artist's conscious attention while he absorbs himself in acting through the inner reality of his reverie, and surrenders to the sensuous pleasure of paint or clay. However, art cannot be achieved by total absorption in immediate sensuous reality, in rapt contemplation of an art work or the tray of shining colours, or the silky bulk of moist clay. At some moment the creative impulse must stretch out the artist's hand and change the inert material, giving visible image to our human need for integration.

Some works are purely abstract but their scale and dramatic impact raises them beyond an effect of mere pattern. Their strange, portentous appearance is greatly enhanced for the onlooker when an image, such as (Figure 4.1) '*Moses*' is created. The transcendence of great Byzantine art is brought to mind, and the sublime simplicities of Cycladic figures, whose very lack of feature seems to preserve them from things mundane.

REVERIE AND FANTASY

The artist watches these works appear from under his hand. (Picasso is said to have remarked, 'I do not seek, I find.') He interferes with the process and the inherent quality of the material as little as possible, withholding conscious skills, recollections, plans. The material may seem to have a life of its own. Henry Moore describes a sense of mystic participation with his material:

> One of the things I would like to think that my sculpture has is a force, is a strength, is a life, a vitality from within it, so that you have a sense that the form is pressing from inside.... It's as though you have something trying to make itself come to a shape from inside itself.   (1966: 60)

The Archaic Linear artist has a certain inertia in fantasy that prevents it from becoming too explicit. This seems due to the immense power of the unconscious reverie in shaping an integrating symbol. Free fantasy is held back, to some extent, to the basic forms that distinguish inner from outer, self from not-self, in the essential proportions. It seems that this fundamental need cannot be sufficiently affirmed and transcends all lesser requirements for associations that would embellish, and enrich or obscure the basic shapes with attributes or representations of outer reality.

THERAPY

When therapy is offered to such a patient the basic problem of integration may not be at all apparent. The superficial effect of drugs can mask a devouring need that I have called the creative impulse. Artists acknowledge it in their work and some can explain something of this in words.

> The serious composer who thinks about his art will sooner or later have occasion to ask himself: why is it so important to my own psyche that I compose music? What makes it seem so absolutely necessary, so that every other daily activity, by comparison, is of lesser significance? And why is the creative impulse never satisfied; why must one always begin anew? ... each added work brings with it an element of self-discovery. I must create in order to know myself, and since self-knowledge is a never-ending search each new work is only a part answer to the question 'Who am I?'.   (Copland 1952: 40–1)

Henry Moore and Aaron Copland both describe the creative process as discovery. The sculptor takes the outside view and finds strength and vitality in the stone as if it were already within: the composer takes the inner view – creating art is discovering himself. His work mirrors the artist as a whole, inside and outside, conscious and unconscious needs.

The Archaic Linear style constellates integration round the core of sensuous dominance, the basic premise of life. This basic problem of identity may be obscured at first by the patient's inability to be spontaneously creative and time has to pass in one way or another before the situation feels safe enough for the patient to concern himself with the fundamental issue, in a relaxation of some safeguards. The sensuous effect of the simple art materials facilitates the withdrawal which Winnicott describes as 'a desultory formless functioning, or perhaps a rudimentary playing as if in a neutral zone' (Winnicott 1971: 64). Perhaps, with utter suddenness, decisive gestures are made that shape Archaic Linear images, to the surprise of the artist and therapist alike. There has been no conscious decision beyond the decision to let go; like floating in water, we can only do it when we are relaxed and know that it is safe to do so. I must be at hand on these occasions in case the force of the image seems overwhelming. I gave an example of this in Chapter 3: a little ball of clay showed Pippi a crack that seemed irremediable.

Years ago some wards in mental hospitals contained patients who had come to live almost entirely in the world of sensuous reality, subduing their powers of thought and intuition to the inner world and cut off from the emotional powers of judgement, like a medieval monk or nun. The psychiatric patients and the artist of the Book of Kells were both protected from external necessity and had time to discover in art images of superhuman order and control. Under certain conditions of therapy such patients could recover a need for the outer world and its complex richness of perceptual stimulation. Edward Adamson has worked for many years to provide a congenial setting where patients can complete free paintings and sculpture. Examples of the perfection of this type of art can be seen in a permanent collection and in his book (Adamson 1984). Other examples of the Archaic Linear style can be found in the drawings of the dancer Nijinsky and also in the late work of the Victorian illustrator Louis Wain.

The changing pattern of psychiatric care reduces the conditions for such expression. This sort of patient in the community may depend for privacy on the narrow bedroom of his family home or a hostel. Also, as we learned from Christopher (Chapter 2), the 'body-self' of sensuous reality may be severely upset by sedatives that create problems of their own. Those individuals who have created and perfected an Archaic Linear image outside a therapeutic milieu may use this image as a last line of defence against disintegration. Then there is little hope of releasing him from his self-hypnosis through art as therapy. From the patient's point of view the therapist is a useless, if not dangerous, imposter, offering a false security that can in no way match the omnipotent power he senses in the archaic image that arrives unbidden whenever he settles down with a pen or paint brush. It may seem crazy to him that he should trust a mere human being to help him.

A word should be said about the intrusive effect of these powerful Archaic images upon the therapist. The aesthetic effect of such elegant works, and the effortless way in which they are made, seems to give them a special authority, and the art therapist may hesitate before such an inspired effect. On the other hand, the therapist may experience a negative projection upon the art work; its potency may seem to make the patient impotent. After struggling to help such a patient over a long period, perhaps of years, we may need to remind ourselves that it is the patient who creates this implacable image – and not the other way round!

I do not know a simple way to offer therapy to such a patient. I can only hang on, waiting until he or she is ready to relinquish the omnipotence of the long-held delusion. Then perhaps I may be able to indicate that the image is a work of art that the patient has made, and can alter, not a ghostly vision that can sustain or devastate him at any moment. Freud describes the outlines of a therapeutic technique in his discussion of the novella *Gravida*

(Freud 1921) in which a eccentric young man is rescued from a delusion by the love and understanding of a young woman. Freud describes this scene as comparable to therapy: 'she accepts her role ... for a short hour, which, she observes, his delusion assigns to her, and in ambiguous words she gently puts him in the way of a new role.' Prinzhorn, the psychiatrist and one-time art student, made a careful study of psychopathological art. He concluded that the basic metaphysical need to create art is the same for all people and made comparisons between the work of psychotic patients, primitives and the art of the great Archaic cultures, as well as those of untaught adults and children. He also investigated the doodles of the bored and fatigued. Alongside the similarities, Prinzhorn found some elements that were peculiar to psychotic arts, such as perseveration, in the sense of meaningless repetition, 'luxuriance of detail' and 'unwillingness to give inherent value to external objects' (Prinzhorn 1972: 19). He noticed the prevailing emphasis on symmetry which he took to be a way of imposing abstract order upon the chaos of the outer world. He believed that the study of symbolism would provide an understanding of all non-naturalistic art, including that of the ancient world, and he looked to the psychoanalytic approaches of Freud and Jung for its future development. Prinzhorn's attitude to psychotic art was sympathetic; he saw it as a valid art form and warned that it would be underestimated if seen merely as another patho-logical symptom. He writes, 'Anybody unable to experience a picture visually without feeling a compulsive desire to explain or unmask it may be a good psychologist but he necessarily bypasses the essence of the creation.' Elsewhere he speaks of the present time as lacking 'that primary experience that precedes all knowledge and which alone produces inspired art'.

Patients may escape the thrall of an image of projected omnipotence in the Archaic Linear style by moving towards the Archaic Massive style in their art, or, in an anticlockwise movement, towards the conceptual world of Traditional Linear art. A young man who had been discharged to a psychiatric day hospital after a prolonged bout of mental illness can be taken as an example of one who moved in the anticlockwise direction. He joined the art group and appeared to enjoy drawing huge faces in the Archaic Linear style. He was very quiet and could easily be overlooked, even in our small group. One day he arrived by car as usual but seemed a little edgy. He took a large sheet of paper (20 × 15 inches), and placed it horizontally on the easel. He painted a design in huge scale which he called 'Petrol pump' (Plate 1.1). The pump had pointed ears which gave it an impression of close attention. The image was placed centrally but shared the paper with a smaller one that echoed the star shape in the motif on the petrol pump. Grinning mischievously, the patient explained that he had awarded the pump a medal for being such a good imitation of a real person (Simon 1975). In this case the placement of the main subject was important, for the image had been made asymmetrical by the addition of the medal. This had the effect of displacing the petrol pump from the central position, and he found in this manoeuvre an effective means of denigrating its effect. The hallucination could enter fantasy through the effect of the pictorial image, and in this way he gained control over it. Kellogg has discussed the symbolism of placement in children's art (Kellogg 1970: 23) and I have found it to be a significant factor in my work with patients, especially those suffering from a psychotic episode, and mentally handicapped adults, and children.

The Archaic Linear style was used by a young woman who came privately to use art as a therapy after leaving hospital. She had usually painted in a Traditional style but made the Archaic Linear painting at a time when her regular sessions had to be interrupted for some months. She countered the startling effect of this painting by naming it – *ECT* (Figure 4.2). She explained many of the ideas that it gave her; the jagged lines of electricity suggested the electro-convulsive treatment of mental disorder, and in many other ways she made good use of the details to look at some of her fears. This prevented her from feeling mad and becoming hypnotized by the sensuous effect of the style. One might say that, in Prinz-

Figure 4.2 *ECT* Archaic Linear

horn's terms, she indicated a compulsive desire to explain or unmask her painting.

Patients who move away from the Archaic Linear style may be exposed to an overwhelming explosion of primitive emotion. For example, Evelyn, a withdrawn, passive young woman who called herself Frank came each week from a long-stay ward to join the hospital art group. She usually painted in the Archaic Linear style, filling large drawings with flat washes of colour, but on this occasion she began to overpaint the original flat blue painting of a head with crimson (Plate 1.2). The mingled colours produced a Massive effect, and when only a small triangle of the original colour remained at the throat she jumped to her feet and brandished a heavy chair. I was nonplussed by this unexpected behaviour but, to my amazement, her emotion was lovingly received by Gertie, another patient who was equally withdrawn most of the time; Gertie steered Evelyn through her mood and eventually walked back to the ward with her. This sympathy and good sense truly reflected the appropriate therapeutic procedure for meeting the patient's emotional state. Gertie had got it right, she could give a

Figure 4.3 *Seaside* Linear Transition

Figure 4.4 *Hospital garden* Archaic Transition

comforting arm because, as she said, 'I know how you feel.' She had responded positively to Evelyn's mood while I had been ineffectively bothered about the reason for her behaviour. In other words, it was the style of the painting rather than the content that constituted its essential message. Later I could see that the overpainting of her static, stylized drawing gave the subject an effect of feminine but negroid features, and uncovered feelings that had previously been contained by the cold perfection and symmetry of the Archaic Linear style.

Mobility within the transitional areas of the Archaic styles will now be discussed in the case of Rosie, an old woman living in a ward for mentally handicapped, psychiatric patients.

Rosie had been attacked by rheumatoid arthritis for some years. Her condition had deteriorated rapidly until she could no longer care for herself. In her state of mind and circumstances she could only be contained in a psychiatric hospital where she was said to spend her time in bitter complaints and cruel tricks upon the staff and patients, who were desperate to get her out of the ward whenever they could. I offered her a place in a weekly group of about nine withdrawn or schizophrenic patients. At first Rosie was very anxious and angry at being moved from the warm ward into the open air and then to an unfamiliar place. The journey in her wheelchair frightened her, she was afraid that I would tip her out, and every broken surface hurt her painful joints. However, once she had arrived she grasped

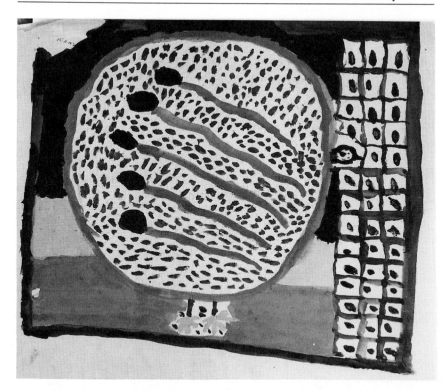

Figure 4.5 *A peacock* Archaic Linear

the opportunity to take the initiative in choosing the colours she wanted. Although her hands were very deformed and weak she took sheets of paper that were almost too large for her to reach across. Rosie knew what she wanted to do. She painted a plan-type view of the seaside resort where she had lived and worked, drawing with a brush in the Linear Transitional style and arranging the coastline in the shape of a quarter circle (Figure 4.3). On the following week Rosie painted a more abstract picture which seemed closer to the Archaic Linear style in a clockwise progression. The drawing, in blue and white, with some pink dots was another plan view, this time of the hospital garden through which we had to pass in the snow to reach the art room (Figure 4.4). Rosie framed this painting and all the others she made over the next few months with a thick boundary line. These plan-type paintings were followed by large-scale pictures of single objects such as the peacock (Figure 4.5), and then her subject matter reflected her anger (Figure 4.6) and self pity. Having made several paintings of this theme her mood changed and she made many paintings of single flowers much larger than life (Figure 4.7). These Archaic Massive paintings reflected a change

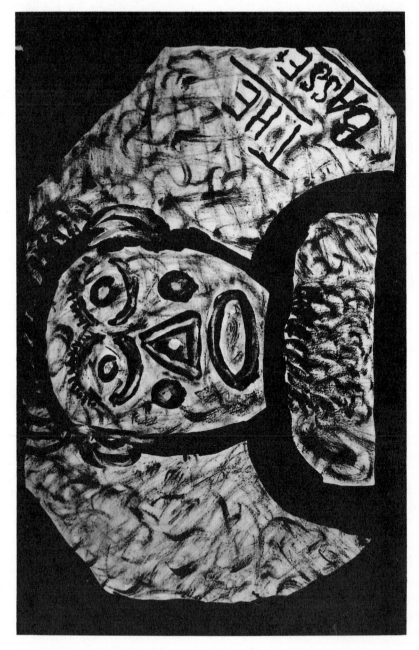

Figure 4.6 *'The Basse'* Archaic Transition

of attitude towards the group; she brought us flowers and sweets that she had stolen from the ward. During the second year her style changed again, she painted birds, butterflies, and flowers in smaller scale, as if she was finding a view of life that was more detached.

THE SYMBOLIC IMAGERY

Rosie's first painting (Figure 4.3) showed that the basic symbol of a circle was conceived unconsciously as being too big to be contained within the square of the pictorial area: only a quarter of it could be shown. This aspect

Figure 4.7 *A rose* Archaic Massive

of herself had remained tied to her past life in the seaside town and, like Pippi's fragmented circle, the image was limited by its conceptual style. However, in her second picture (Figure 4.4) she moved closer to sensuous reality in an abstract pattern based on the hospital garden. She painted complete circles, segmented like a wheel with spokes. The symbolic meaning could be compared with Pippi's concern with identical pairs and the imaging of the sense of a split between inner and outer reality. Such preoccupations lead on to primitive feelings which may have been expressed by the pink dots on the white circle and the thick black line surrounding the other one.

Rosie's next move towards integration led to the painting of a large, Archaic Linear circle of self which was given the attributes of a peacock (Figure 4.5). These attributes are only slightly extended beyond the circle, as a head and feet; however, they enable the symbolic image to be extended, connecting the squares on the left of the painting to the circle in terms of the possibility of 'food' being within reach, set out in an organized way. After this, the images of the Archaic Linear style were given up and Rosie could paint her body as human and mourn for its suffering. In a painting she called 'The Basse' (Figure 4.6) Rosie used black to show a human being for the first time. It is seen degraded, without the life of colour. Later, she made a diagram of her mutilated body and wrote on it the details of every ache and pain. In this Archaic Linear painting her style

Figure 4.8 *Birds* Massive Transition

moved anticlockwise a little as she added the written words and attempted a rational interpretation of her suffering. In this case the pictorial image of sensuous experience led her to think about it. This led to positive feelings as well and she reflected emotional reality in huge paintings of flowers such as the rose in Figure 4.7. Her recovery did not end there for her style continued to develop. The scale became smaller and in paintings such as the picture of birds she included representations that showed a greater awareness of shared reality (Figure 4.8). In the last painting shown here (Figure 4.9) Rosie achieved a sense of distance which I term 'stage and backdrop', to be discussed in detail in Chapter 7 as a feature of the Massive Transitional style.

In summary this chapter refers to the dominance of sensuous reality as the *raison d'être* underlying the Archaic Linear style. As an expression of primal reality integrating inner and outer life it can have immense power over a weakened sense of self. The positive aspect of this basic symbolism lies in its containing and ordering (symmetrical) effect, but if the image perseverates the artist may be led into a state of hypnotic fusion and lose his self in an image that seems to be an omnipotent other.

Figure 4.9 *An orchard* Massive Transition

Figure 5.1 *Emerging from chaos* Archaic Transition

Chapter 5

The Archaic Transition
From feelings to emotions

This chapter develops the idea of a transition between the Archaic Linear and Massive styles of art. Within the overlap between these styles we can discern some qualities that are unique; they will be discussed in detail, particularly in their relevance to therapy.

THE APPEARANCE

Archaic works that reflect the general area of transition will show both Linear and Massive elements to some extent. These may blend smoothly; for instance, when lines overlay or contain mass; or indicate special attributes of a shape. Mass may be kept separate from line, as in *The witch girl* (Figure 2.3): the mass of the girl's red hair being separate from the linear drawing of her face.

There are other paintings where mass and line do not work together; in fact they cancel out each other's effectiveness, disrupting the unity of the picture. Such work appears fragmented and chaotic, having a marked diagonal emphasis. The mass of muddled colours that overflowed the circle in Pippi's painting (Figure 3.7) of the mop and the spider's web is an example.

POSTURE AND GESTURE

The grace and elegance of the Archaic Linear artist is converted into the energetic brush-work of Archaic mass during the stage of transition, reflected more or less in the quality of the overpainting and the vibrancy of the colours. In works where line and mass conflict, they are characteristically diagonal and confused.

REVERIE AND FANTASY

Works that indicate an equable transition between Linear and Massive Archaic styles seem to arise smoothly during a state of reverie and fantasy, developing from the motor pleasure of using line and mass. However, there seems little coherent fantasy in the area of maximum overlay between the styles and, like Pippi's early sessions, the patient's excitement can prevent him from settling down or losing himself in reverie for some time until his creative needs can be focused upon an art material.

THE SYMBOLIC IMAGERY OF THE STYLE

The Archaic Linear style reflects the basic sensuousness and motor pleasure of creativity as its dominant aspect. Normally, sensuous feelings during art work are in association with emotions that refer to the content, which can be recognized in the subject matter of the work. However, when there is a block in this natural flow towards the emotional aspect of feelings, a break-through of primitive emotion disturbs the scale and symmetry of the Archaic Linear style, introducing an effect of diagonal emphasis which may lead to incoherence and chaotic effects. In some cases diagonals may obtrude in an otherwise symmetrical work, indicating a movement away from sensuous dominance towards emotional realization. These changes in style can apply to the work of patients of all ages and is particularly signifi-cant when the Archaic Linear style is habitual; they indicate a progressive thrust, or when the Archaic Massive style is the usual one; then a thera-peutic regression is indicated, a need to withdraw from emotional commit-ment, at least for a time. An example of therapeutic regression of this sort can be seen in Rowanna's paintings (Figures 5.2 and 5.3).

FAILURE TO INTEGRATE SENSUOUS AND EMOTIONAL REALITY

An ability to use the transitional area between any two styles is a feature of mental health. It indicates a flexible attitude to life that can respond posi-tively to different points of view. Within the whole area of Archaic Tran-sition there are countless degrees of emphasis between the sensuous qualities of the Archaic Linear style that are tempered or extended by the emotional strength of Archaic colour and mass. However, works that are fragmented, diagonal and chaotic reflect the patient's inability to formulate a consistent sense of reality. He is neither able to believe the truth of his senses nor his emotional evaluation: he is exposed to anxiety and confusion. Classically, this confusion is linked with sexual frustration arising from the split between sensuous and emotional components of desire.

In this mental state, which may be either temporary or habitual, the boundary of the self is fragmented, as we saw in 'The Big I' (Figure 3.6).

The patient cannot refer his sensations to the inside or outside of his body. His emotions may also feel dislocated, or oscillating so rapidly that he doubts the validity of each. One patient described his excitement as 'dancing on a threepenny bit', and such a dance of emotions can seem orgiastic and exasparating to the patient's carers. This excitement could explain the readiness that these patients show for art work and also their difficulty in becoming deeply involved in it to the extent that a unified form can be made.

When mental conflict of this sort has become an illness, the patient is forced to defend himself by rationalizing its effects. This may create an illusion that the patient's body is damaged, or extraordinary in some way. Such a projection of the whole self upon the body seems to have the effect of dismembering the mind as if it were a pile of bricks – the bottom brick giving way and the rest having to fall. This trite analagy is not without use if it indicates the interdependence of mental functions and the basic distinction between inner and outer reality as the first essential for our sanity. Without the boundary line of the circle in the square, all is chaos. Mental and physical pain are interchangeable and hurt to the mind is felt as hurt to the head. A patient helped me to understand this confusion when she described herself as having 'a sort of phantom limb, half torn from the bone'. I could follow the metaphor for her painting was made in diagonal red and blue stripes, somewhat reminiscent of thigh muscles. She had fragmented the visual image and also her description – as a *sort* of phantom that was *only half* attached to the bone. Yet I had an impression of excruciating pain that could not be felt with full emotional impact. It was clear to me that, as she said, she needed 'bandaging'. A patient's efforts to care for the imagined damage felt in his body may be elaborated in ways that seem bizarre. Pippi (Chapter 3) had the spastic gait that expressed his unbalance between sensuous and emotional reality. In some cases an actual, or past disability may be woven into the delusion, as in the case of Rosie (Chapter 4) who had equated her bad feelings with her arthritic body. While such a delusion is held in the patient's mind it evidently cannot be influenced by external reality.

THERAPEUTIC MOVEMENT

Winnicott is extraordinarily helpful in describing the patients' need in this state. In the chapter entitled 'The search for self' he describes the need for 'rudimentary playing' in an unintegrated state and the need for it to be reflected back to the patient. He goes on to say: 'This gives us our indication for therapeutic procedure – to afford an opportunity for formless experience, and for creative impulses, motor and sensory, which are the stuff of playing' (Winnicott 1971: 64).

The spontaneous use of art materials in the presence of the art therapist does, I think, allow such an unintegrated state to be reflected back to the patient through his art work, which has been preceded by a destruction of form. The flat surface of the paper is symbolically broken when marks are made upon it and the mass of clay is broken into or flattened when it is handled. Some patients feel this destructiveness quite violently; for example, a young woman threw a tray of powder colours upside down upon a sheet of white paper and smeared it with wet fingers. She called the result *The Destruction of Evolution*. Similarly, the Incredible Hulk, who will be discussed later in the chapter, played out this preparatory destruction with a clay puddle. The value of providing the simplest art materials such as paint and clay cannot be overestimated as a means of recording the need to undo, regress and destroy in safety. Destruction and transformation through art materials is an innate part of the creative impulse and in the silent, receptive atmosphere of the therapy room this unintegrated state can draw upon the depths of mindless reverie. That which I describe as art work may indeed become an elementary form of play at this time, the art materials may be used in a very unorthodox way. Some people seem to use them to regress to fantasies of primal omnipotence in which a baby is imagined to create everything and have total power over his creations.

Images of spitting or shitting occur and are usually contained within the art work but sometimes may be acted out (Schaverien 1987). An adult or child may grind his bottom into his painting, and in one case a woman could completely regurgitate into her cup all the tea that she had just swallowed. In such ways the need to undo appears to precede the integrated state described by Winnicott. In the studio, time must be held for the patient's unconscious reverie, his withdrawal into smearing, acting out or mute inactivity. Some creative works may be made very rapidly indeed, but the reverie cannot be hurried.

After a period of apparently aimless activity, the patient often reintegrates on the sensuous level – that is, through the Archaic Linear style; this is an anticlockwise movement in the circle of styles (Figure 1.1). In this style the boundary between self and other, inner and outer reality, is clearly defined and given order and symmetry. Pippi's art work is a case in point. When he had settled down enough to paint at all he drew an Archaic Linear circle that was dangerously fragmented and invaded by the 'square' of his inflated ego – the Big I. After that painting he could become absorbed in formless experience, messing with art materials, and meaningless conjuring tricks. Some children seem to symbolize the need for destruction and transformation by using paint only to colour the paint water; then, when the paint is used on paper the symbolism moves beyond the act to the image. I presume that this is what Hanna Segal means by the difference between symbolic equivalence and the symbol proper (Segal 1986: 195). She gives a beautiful example in which a patient says: 'When you name a thing you really lose it.' Segal comments that the patient could then see that using a symbol (language) meant the acceptance of the separateness of her object from herself. Pippi transformed the feather duster from a symbolic equivalent to a true symbol by painting it.

An established delusion, as a defence against intolerable pain, seems more common in hospitalized patients than in those who remain outside. In hospital, such patients are almost always sedated, which protects them from becoming exhausted by excitement, but although the delusion is contained within reasonable limits, the effect of the treatment may add to the delusion; for example, Chris's homosexual fantasies (Chapter 2) were reinforced, if not created, by the extra fat he gained in hospital as a result of sedation.

When a patient sees his delusion imaged in a work of spontaneous art, it is a critical moment. He is face to face with the integrative demands of the whole self as it exists in inner and outer reality. Such moments of insight can seem extraordinary, and reach far beyond anything that another person could offer. They might also seem precarious because, to the outsider, an image of a delusion might seem to confirm it for the patient. I have not, myself found this happen but it might occur if the image was interpreted prematurely so that the symbol was sundered from its outer manifestation. Although the creation of an image of a delusion can lead to its resolution, the process may take time to have an appreciable effect. In the case of the Incredible Hulk, presented later in this chapter, there is a beautiful example of time being taken to make a delusion conscious through repetitive play.

Two examples follow which show clearly the conflict between an over-whelming sensuous perception of reality and the primitive emotions that misinterpret it. The result of such conflict might be defined as a madness brought on by intolerable pain, which is displaced from the mind to the body. The patients' symptoms reflected their efforts to avoid physical death as the final failure of inner reality. The cases are comparable in their use of the Archaic Transitional style but different in the degree to which their madness affected their lives. The woman had an extensive delusion that had brought her into psychiatric hospital, while the child's delusion, though developing rapidly, was still localized and he could be contained in his own home. The treatment of adult psychotic patients like Rowanna has changed many times since I met her more than twenty years ago, but the presenting symptoms are probably familiar to workers on the acute wards. The problem of the violent child in the second example is still with us.

THE CONTRIBUTION OF THE STYLE IN THERAPY

Rowanna, a lady of about forty, joined the hospital art group in a wheel-chair, tormented by the delusion that she had become someone else who was crippled. She had bandaged each of her fingers and was convinced that she could not walk or raise her arms. Nevertheless, she was eager to paint and chose to have the chair wheeled to an easel rather than a more comfortable place at a table. In spite of the difficulties of her position, she made a painting on paper 15 × 12 inches, using diagonal brush-strokes of red and green paint, filling the main area with forceful lines which were finally overlaid with white and two lozenge shapes, filled with lines of paint (Figure 5.2). Rowanna's excitement led her to duplicate many of her gestures but, in spite of many layers of paint, the picture is not smeared, although the overall effect is chaotic. I noticed the sensuous grace with which the brush-work was made, and the rich colouring contained within a white margin. In terms of basic symbolism the painting suggested that Rowanna responded to the paper as a containing square, while the circle of self appeared to be duplicated in the lozenge shape and could have had the attributes of a veiled eye.

In her next session Rowanna painted again, this time first using a black

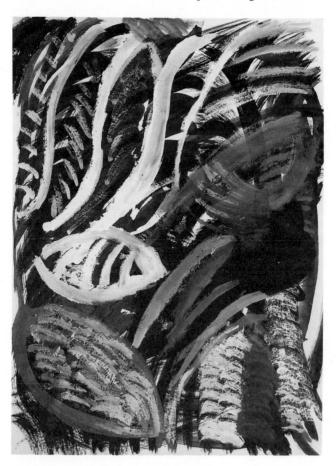

Figure 5.2 *Chaos* Archaic Transition

scribble of diagonal painted lines. These she roughly organized into a head by overpainting areas with masses of red and purple paint which gave an effect of a turnip head joined to a neck or body (Figure 5.1). The lozenge shapes that appeared in Figure 5.2 were imposed upon this form, their placement and attributes now indicating that they are meant to suggest a mouth and eyes.

Later, when Rowanna was giving up her delusion of a crippled body, her pictorial style changed in an anticlockwise direction: the scale became huge and her work showed the characteristic symmetry of the Archaic

Figure 5.3 *'The sacred vessel'* Archaic Linear

Linear style. However, she continued to use the same vivid colours for the flat infilling of the linear shapes, rather than the lighter shades that are typical of the Archaic Linear style. In this painting, called '*The sacred vessel*' (Figure 5.3), the decoration gave the impression of a strange face with screwed-up eyes and large ears. It seemed to have two mouths: a red lozenge shape forming an angry grimace and another mouth above it, painted in blue lines, suggesting a smile that shows the teeth. Neither Rowanna nor I spoke about the strange effect of a face. In the third style, shown by the painting of a volcano (Figure 5.4), the work was mainly Archaic Massive: the subject was central, symmetrical and convex, the colours rich and strong. However, the background was not typical of the Archaic Massive style, for it gave an impression of receding space. The painting was the last that Rowanna made and it seemed that she was already looking beyond the basic symbolism of self and other integration in terms of emotional verity, and was moving towards a more objective relation to life.

Rowanna's painting styles inform us of the way in which she recovered. Her first paintings showed a violent undoing of whole objects, form and shape within a limited pictorial space which she indicated by the boundary or margin left round the edge of her painting. The gestural freedom she used in making these works must, I think, have contributed to the undermining of the delusion, but it was the affirmation of her right to formless experience in art that seems to have allowed her to make a therapeutic regression to the sensuous dominance of images such as the sacred vessel and then forwards round the circle of styles to full emotional realization implicit in the volcano painting. The rich colour in all her work indicated a strong core of emotional realization that had conflicted with the demands of that sensuous life.

In paintings such as '*The sacred vessel*', Rowanna could move beyond the delusion of physical disability and temporarily integrate through sensuous transcendance. We might tentatively interpret to ourselves the volcano painting as the discovery of an illuminating metaphor: a down-to-earth image of the self in the foreground, erupting, so she told me, with glorious energy and brilliant, red-hot lava, in the vicinity of other, quiescent volcanoes that could only cast dark shadows into the sky. The self symbol in this picture is a triangle, a version of the square; the self circle is modified by outer needs, but by her incorporation of the background we might see forecast a more flexible relation of self to other contained in a consistent image of space.

My final example of the value of the Archaic Transition is drawn from therapeutic work with the Incredible Hulk, a six-year-old boy whose use of clay enabled him to relinquish an habitual attitude of defensive visual thinking and then to uncover the emotional needs that had been blocked by amnesia. I will return to this interesting child in Chapter 10 to show how

Figure 5.4 *The volcano* Archaic Massive

this visual thinking expressed his difficulties and also helped him to deal with them.

The child's parents had been divorced for several years and the father no longer visited the family. Although the Hulk had been very upset by the violence that preceded the divorce, he now seemed to have forgotten all about it but told people that his father was dead. It was said that he no longer recognized his father if they accidently met in the street. Although the Hulk was a loving and helpful son, well liked by his teachers, he would suddenly attack any boy or man without reason, hitting and kicking them, or throwing sticks or stones. He could not be trusted to play in the street or the school playground, and his mother was horrified to see him once trying to push a child in front of a moving bus. Moreover, she said, at times he would suddenly go 'beserk' at home and attack her; she had been forced to beat him for this, but this deeply distressed her for he did not understand the punishment and cried 'Mummy, you don't love me.' When his grandmother asked him why he was cruel to the dog, he said that it was to make it cry.

When I first met this bright, wiry little boy he was keen to come and paint. He first showed me that he was used to paint at school and offered to make some similar hand- and foot-prints in various colours. The final colour he chose was a pale, jade green – the sort of colour that children usually ignore. However, he was very excited when he saw this colour on his hands and demanded to show his mother that he was the Incredible Hulk, a fictitious character from a television serial, in which an essentially good and kind young man is temporarily transformed into a pale green giant if faced with evidence of injustice. I was impressed by the skill with which the Hulk manoeuvred the door open without getting the paint from his hands spread about.

The Hulk spent the next six sessions painting pictures himself at home or at school and making copies of the patterns knitted into the front of his jumpers. At the same time that he was delighted by making these self images, he acted out his violence by attacking the tall cupboard in my room, crashing the metal door repeatedly and offering to break it for me. In the eighth session he found some soft clay, handling it at first rather timidly and expressing some fear that it might make him dirty. Soon he discovered that clay could be squeezed in water to make mud, and he poured this sludge into the middle of the table until it flowed to the very edge. When it threatened to overflow I silently offered a sponge, which he used with grace and skill to clean off the edges of the table and control the flood. His deftness in handling the potentially destructive aspect of paint and clay assured me of the vitality of his sensuous life, which did not seem to be damaged by his conflict in the way that Pippi, for instance, had been fragmented.

The Hulk began to build an elaborate hill in the centre of this muddy mess, piling up the clay into a circular mound, then, using a short dowel, he bored two holes in the side. He was sexually excited by this, repeatedly thrusting the dowelling into the clay; then he forced the rod into the top of the clay hill. He asked for my help in steadying it while he added some rough, unfashioned pieces of clay to the top, shouting that he was making a hat and ears for the monster. When I asked him why a monster should be on the end of a dowel the Hulk shouted that it was not a dowel but a pole, a telephone-post pole and I must ask the monster if I wanted to know why it was there. I took a piece of clay and quickly made something like a telephone and the monster told me that the telephone pole was broken. When I asked him who had broken it the monster shouted that I had done this myself. I then asked who would pay for all the hard work of repairing it – would the monster have to pay? Of course not, said the Hulk.

The Hulk was enchanted with this story and said that we should repeat it to his mother, exactly.

This drama was repeated during the next three sessions. I did not altogether understand its significance but thought roughly in terms of the hill being the parents' bed and the monster, as a substitute for the Hulk's hand, destroying it. This led me to the idea of reparation, by asking who would mend the pole. However, although this view of unconscious guilt was broadly correct, the play also referred to a specific trauma that I did not know at the time. During the following weeks the story became slightly modified. The Hulk renamed the monster, 'the giant', and I added an apology for breaking the pole. He omitted the preliminary work of making the hill and the tunnels after the second replay. Further, when I asked again who was going to pay for the damage to the pole the Hulk replied rather grandly that he would.

After the Christmas break it seemed that the story had been forgotten but during the fourteenth session the Hulk came up and leaned against me, asking if I remembered it. He asked me to tell him the story as he did not want to make it with the clay. I was not quite sure what value my retelling of the story would have; so I said that I did not remember all of it but that if he would tell the story to me I would write it down and read it back to him. He was pleased with this idea and, as so often happens, the story developed in the retelling:

> Once upon a time the Incredible Hulk found somebody up the telephone pole. He said to him, 'Incredible Hulk, can I come and scare you?' So the Incredible Hulk said, 'Get away and don't come back again.'

In this remarkable recapitulation we can see the boy's recovery from amnesia. His grandmother told me later that when the Hulk was four years old he had answered the telephone and used these words to his father. After this session the Incredible Hulk recognized his father when they happened to meet, and, according to his grandmother, he said, 'I know who you are, you're Peter. Why don't you come and visit us?'

INTERVENTION AND PLAY

Although I see art as a therapy essentially created by the patient in the presence of a therapist, and am very wary of introducing my own creative material, there are occasions when, if I were to withhold active participation it would seem rejecting, and interrupt the patient's creative impulse. This is particularly true when children assign a role to me in play. I take it up as far as possible within the limits indicated by the child. However, there are some occasions when my contribution might be based upon issues that seem hidden from the child, or at least not expressed in the play. My question 'who will pay?' is a case in point. This differs from a direct interpretation because it offers my extension of the play obliquely, as part of the story, that the child can use or ignore, according to his immediate level of need.

To my view of art therapy there is always a danger in relying too much on the actual words that are spoken in a session. They easily shed their symbolic associations and become transformed into literal meaning that clogs the therapeutic process, whether the words are used to reflect upon art work or dramatic play. Therapy is an art, and as such transcends rational boundaries: its leaps and hesitances, perhaps most of all the quality of its silences all go to make up the facilitations that occur. My intuitions during mutual play can be followed or abandoned without loss of rapport with the patient if they are enacted, but remain unverbalized. If I always included a description of my responses in this text they would appear tortuous and confusing, yet visual communication is usually more apt, flexible and companionable, although less precise than words. Winnicott (1971: 86) distinguishes between making interpretations to a patient and interpreting, as a means of therapeutic understanding.

The foregoing excerpts from therapeutic work with the Incredible Hulk have been given to show his and my stages of progress in understanding one part of his problem – the amnesia. In no way could I have led him to this understanding. This is not to say that I came without any skill or experience that could be drawn upon but that such knowledge is general and, by relying on it, could easily distract my attention from what was actually going on. It is important to keep this past experience far back in the corner of my conscious mind. My immediate task is to recognize the symbolic, pregnant expression apart from the habitual reaction. I need to follow the generative process of symbolic imaging. To do this, the patient's habitual reactions may need to be curbed, as when Pippi was prevented from running all over my house.

Play with paint or clay seems to me more potent than play with found objects, such as tables and chairs, toys or feather brooms. These have not been made from formless material and although they may be the focus of a patient's projections, acting as a painting or claywork as a focal point, yet the object is to some extent more limited, carrying traces of its meaning in outer reality that can distort or diminish the symbolism. Moreover, outer reality may claim the object and unwittingly reinforce the patient's projection. The Hulk's attack on the cupboard is a case in point. The cupboard can first be seen as a symbol of the square, the 'not-me' and alien to himself. It was tall, hard and inflexible – taller than either of us – and he offered to break it for me, his playfellow. I thought the cupboard might have some attributes of his father, whose desertion of the family aroused his destructiveness. As the Hulk had deluded himself into thinking that his father was dead, some of the attack might be to keep his father dead, and to compulsively open and shut the door in order to also look inside to see if he was destroyed or not.

I was not afraid that the Hulk would damage himself – or the steel cupboard – but the noise he made was too disturbing to the staff in adjoining rooms and so I was forced to intervene. This gave me a lot of thought, for I realized that if I treated the cupboard non-symbolically, as only a cupboard, and the noise only as a noise I would not only interfere with the Hulk's symbolic imagery but I would destroy his faith in me as a playfellow and become attacked as one who challenged the introjected Daddy. The Hulk might go 'beserk' on me and we would fight physically, as his Mummy and Daddy had fought. I would have to win physically in restraining him and then I would lose him as a friend. By locking the cupboard and giving him access to the key I hoped to contain his need to control the cupboard in a quieter way. The success of this intervention was measured by the fact that the Hulk made a very positive extension of this idea.

It was clear that the Hulk saw the cupboard as a foe to be attacked, and when I locked it I suppose it had also become an image of rejection. I later understood that his need to control the cupboard linked in with his need to get the good thing that had been lost when he had told his father to go away, and made him 'dead'. This good thing was, in fact, an ability to separate out from his introjected father. Possession of the key seemed to me a means of self-possession, and the Hulk continued for some weeks to unlock the cupboard when he arrived. If it was unlocked, the Hulk first locked it and then at the end of the session he locked it again and returned the keys to my desk with a flourish. Symbolic play was also enacted when the clay puddle threatened to flow on to the floor. The Hulk was testing the limits of his control over the self. If I had interfered directly, rather than just handing him a sponge, he would have had an opportunity to go beserk and succumb to the introjected monster-daddy or project it upon me. The difference between the cupboard incident and the clay puddle incident lies in the quality of the intervention. In the first case I had a strategy, while in the second I responded intuitively for, by that time, we had got to know each other.

In summary, the Archaic Transition is seen as an image of conflict between sensuous and emotional reality. My work with patients such as Rowanna and the Incredible Hulk led me to distinguish their delusions as symbolic equivalents rather than true symbolic manifestations that could weld discrete experiences into a single meaning. The force of these delusions seems to be introjectory – Rowanna felt herself to be someone else and the Hulk was 'beside himself' when he was beserk, feeling himself change as did the Incredible Hulk in the film.

In therapy, art creations provide the images of destruction of evolution that are needed. By 'stepping back in order to leap forward', the Hulk could put aside the learned skill and control he used in painting and use clay to show the destructiveness that precedes creation of the individual self. The monster was made up of unidentifiable fragments rather than an adopted film hero, and out of this willed confusion came a coherent story that reached back into the trauma of the telephone conversation two years before, when his sensuous excitement of rough and tumble games with his father had become so threatening that the Hulk had been forced to 'make him dead'.

Figure 6.1 *Pig face* Archaic Massive

Chapter 6

The Archaic Massive style
Emotional reality

We come now to consider in detail the appearance of art work that I describe as Archaic Massive. I shall follow this with an interpretation of the symbolic meaning that its images present although I cannot hope to avoid some oversimplification and distortion in imposing inflexible soundless words upon visual images. Any work of art can seem a dull and boring catalogue of ideas when described in cold prose, even if it is in fact appealing and immediately meaningful to the eye. I will also take up the idea of art as a spontaneous therapy that may sometimes appear outside the clinical situation.

We can hardly overestimate the importance of creating art for patients whose self-image has been confronted with damage to their body by physical illness or handicap. Although it is generally accepted that such experiences should be worked through, the fear, horror, rage and disgust cannot always be expressed and therapeutic time may not be available for the work of acceptance and assimilation. Patients who have been mutilated have a desperate need to be held by the strength of their emotional integrity. Without this firm inner core patients may regress to chaotic confusion, such as that which we saw imaged in the Archaic Transitional style. Alternatively, they may block off all emotion. I have found that the spontaneous creation of Archaic Massive images can focus the resources of such patients.

THE APPEARANCE

The essential qualities that distinguish the Archaic Massive style in the art of adults and children are its large-scale and vibrant colours which give an effect of convexity and weight to simple forms. Secondary features are seen in the symmetry that persists from the Archaic Linear style which in this art is overlaid by masses that sometimes modify it (Figure 6.1). The precursors of the style can be found in the earliest art of children, which I will briefly reiterate. Scribbled lines, which are woven and accidentally impacted in parts of a drawing become focal points which add colour/tone to the drawing and give an effect of solidity and concentrated energy.

This style develops the effectiveness of colour more fully than any other style. No colour is neutral for each, in a way, affects the others. Each colour added to a painting acts like a magnet to attract or repel the boundaries of its neighbours. Colours seem to expand or contract but also suggest a relation to the picture plane, receding back from the surface if cool or surging forward sometimes, as if they had broken through the surface altogether. Colours optically 'leak' in this way and the Archaic Massive artist responds to these effects unthinkingly. It is fascinating to watch such an artist working; both adults and children frequently change the shapes and colours by overpainting, or modify them with smears or dots of another colour. Unthinkingly they pursue the shifting colour values of the work until a harmonious balance is obtained. Even when a painting is made directly, and unaltered (Figure 6.5, for instance) we see the vitality of the colours giving an effect of massive form pressing beyond the outlines.

Expressionism is a recent version of Archaic Massive art. It is rooted in subjective experience, reaching beyond the limits of representation to the emotional reality felt by the painter for his subject. Rouault and Georg Grosz can affect us intensely through the colour and texture of the painted forms. These artists worked in a culture which accepted Archaic as well as Traditional art, but in the days of the artist Peter Paul Rubens the Archaic quality was modified by the tenets of classical art. In his case I imagine that this blend of subjective and objective expression coincided with a popular attitude for he was completely successful in his integrations of inner and outer reality, bringing the Archaic qualities of convexity and weight to post-Renaissance naturalism. His vigorous brush-strokes sweep across the satin and flesh of the painted women, convincing us that the rapacious soldiers are lifting 16, 18 or 20 stones of flesh as they struggle to carry off the Sabine women, who do little to help or hinder them. The Archaic values of mass and form may also appear in abstract art. In times nearer our own, Mark Rothko weaves a visual spell in vast canvasses that appear to sustain the forward thrust of colour by surface tension, like a pool full to the top and nearly brimming over.

REVERIE

The act of creating is accomplished in a mood of withdrawal that I term reverie. In the Archaic Massive style reverie is constellated by colours and their abstract effect upon each other. It seems that colours, appearing without linear design, unconsciously symbolize the quality of emotional integration. Some adult and child patients find the effect of abstract colour meaningful enough, and do not add the attributes of fantasies or represent images. Therapists who believe that conscious comprehension of unconscious content is always essential may feel that such patients are evasive or wasting time in 'no-paintings' (Betensky 1973: 349). Once we become sensitive to the meaning of art styles we can appreciate the integrative effect of colour as a symbol of self/other relation, which the patient's eye and hand have experienced. He may then come to employ the sensitivity that has been awakened by colour in emotional realizations referring to other areas of his life (Betensky 1973: 143).

FANTASY

The reverie, though essentially unconscious, is often extended in fantasies developed from the abstract shapes and colours. Fantasies may also develop as stories or recollections.

THE SYMBOLISM OF THE STYLE

The style of an art work symbolizes its meaning. We have only to translate the way a spontaneous work of art is made to understand why one particular style and no other came to be used. Each style is seen to symbolize a particular attitude towards reality as it is experienced at the time. With the creation of a symbolic image the artist makes the accompanying attitude visible. Of course no attitude is wrong in itself but it may be out of date or otherwise inappropriate. Spontaneous art as therapy invites the birth of new attitudes.

The Archaic Massive style can be described in visual terms as solid-looking and convex, immediate and vivid. These qualities reflect the artist's habitual attitude to life or his transient mood, only evoked, at first, in some cases by the motor pleasure of creative activity. Only a sequence of paintings can show the durability of the style and the importance of its underlying attitude in the patient's life. The florid, dynamic use of colour that is unique to the Archaic Massive style demands our attention. We may warm to these passionate paintings or, in a different mood, recoil in dismay from their primitive violence. These reactions to images of 'unbridled emotion' reflects the difficulty that a sensuous or a thinking attitude meets in the presence of emotional reality. Milner (1986: 24) explicitly describes this when she speaks of 'a feeling for colour as something moving and alive in its own right, not fixed and bound like the colouring of a map'. She reminds us of:

> an unknown fear to be encountered in this matter of colour and the plunge into full imaginative experience of it – to part of my mind the changing world seemed near to a mad one and the fixed world the only sanity. And this idea of there being no fixed outline, no boundary between one state and another also introduced the idea of no boundary between one self and another self, it brought in the idea of one personality merging with another.

Archaic massive art expresses value judgements. It appeals to our need to divide the good from the bad and reconcile them through the power of art. This may affect the content – so that we can enjoy the ugly rape of the Sabine women – but this attitude is also expressed in the style, which is our main concern here. When emotion is given an image, the whole area of feeling is activated. Formless emotion is given shape that is distinct from its physical, sensuous effect – as we saw in Rosie's art (Figure 4.6). Emotion can also be distinguished from intuitive modifications or contaminations, as Chris discovered in his painting of *The witch girl* (Figure 2.3). Thus, at some moment during art work the emotion becomes an object and, to some extent objectified. Confused feeling has been contained in the circle in the square. This basic symbol affirms the style in relation with the other, and in this style the self is present, as passionate and interactive through colour and massive form.

The colours and forms in Archaic Massive present a paradox. As symbolic images they are both loved and hated; that is, loved things can be given hated colour, and hated things can be loved for the beauty of their form. Beautiful things are ugly and ugly things beautiful; bad things can be good and good ones bad. Rowanna's destructive volcano erupted with 'glorious energy' (Figure 5.4). These opposites, which are easily contained in the symbolic imagery of the primary process are laborious to write and to read, but they appear instantly comprehensible to the eye when we create Archaic Massive art or respond to it in the work of a patient. One patient in an angry mood chose colours she disliked and, in using them discovered that they were beautiful. This discovery was a very important message to herself.

THE STYLE IN THERAPY

The spontaneous creation of an image of emotion brings it into consciousness and gives it form in the symbolism of the circle in the square. The activity required to bring this work about affirms the value of the emotion and uses it. As a result, the need for its recognition is met and extended beyond the primitive impulse of expression, as I saw when Gertie understood the painting of the *Red head* (Plate 1.2).

Patients who suffer disunity between their body and its self-image may experience an actual disability – such as Rosie's rheumatoid arthritis – or a delusional one, as in Rowanna's case (Chapter 5). Winnicott (1971: 66) is very helpful in describing these confusing states:

they may not be firmly structured in respect of the psycho-somatic partnership so that they are said to have poor coordination. Sometimes a physical disability such as defective sight or hearing plays into this state of affairs making a confused picture in which one cannot clearly distinguish between an hallucinating state and a disability based ultimately on a physical abnormality. In the extreme of this state of affairs the person being described is a patient in a mental hospital, either temporarily or permanently, and is labelled schizophrenic.

Winnicott emphasizes that in these graduated states 'we find clinically *no sharp line* between health and the schizoid state or even between health and full-blown schizophrenia'.

Terry had been blind for 12 years. Four operations on his eyes, when he was 12 years old had not saved his failing sight and from that time his mental health deteriorated until psychiatric help was needed. After some months he was discharged to the social services and attended mobility classes for the blind, but he could not follow instructions or walk without physical contact with another person. He continued to show strange mannerisms, including inappropriate giggling and spitting. He seemed unable to use his hands even to feed himself properly and his family found it very difficult to live with him. He was offered individual sessions of art therapy for an hour each week and used paint, clay and creative writing.

Terry's fear of using his hands appeared to be linked to a fear of messing or dirtying himself. However, I noticed that he was an extremely messy eater and his food would be over the table, his clothes, his face and his hands. When introducing the art materials I offered Terry an overall and bought a nail brush and after a while he began to be interested in the idea of painting, even though he could see nothing at all, and proved this to me by removing his dark glasses and asking me to tell him what I saw of the damage to his eyes. Then he made some paintings with thick gouache on the basis of the colours he described and I mixed for him. These were mainly red and blue, occasionally green. He smeared these colours thickly over large sheets of paper without attempting to create a shape. He showed no interest in keeping within the edges of the paper but his gestures seemed to express the 'destruction of evolution'. Then he turned to clay, and after initial hesitance hit and chopped at it with wooden tools, which he called knives. Like Pippi, he enjoyed thrusting the dowel into the top of the clay and wanted to take some of these pieces home. Contrary to my usual feeling that the art work should remain with me until the end of therapy, and because I knew how much the family would be encouraged to see that Terry had 'made something', I had one of these curious pieces fired and he gave it to his mother as a stand to hold cut flowers in a dish! Terry later made some more conventional pieces, such as a naturalistic model of a dog that once he had owned.

In the next phase I offered my services as secretary to write stories to his dictation and then to read them back to him. However, he admitted that he could type and began to compose poems and stories, first based on child-hood recollections of the time when he had friends and was adjusted to minimal sight. He recalled a dangerous adventure that he had met with courage. Then he was drawn to more recent times, when the family moved from the country during his stay in hospital. He spoke bitterly of this period: of going into hospital with little sight and coming out with none, of the strange surroundings of his new home, and of having to thank the doctors and nurses for making him blind.

As Terry created these feelings in stories and poems he gave up his mannerisms and could make use of the mobility training. He learned to use a white stick and walk alone to a social club where he could meet young people.

Terry made good use of art therapy in a remarkably short time, attending once a week for just over a year. His return to health seemed surprisingly uncomplicated, particularly as he had seemed to have a schizophrenic illness of long, slow development. Evidently it is possible for people such as Terry to recover their mental equilibrium through the un-directed use of art materials in the situation of individual therapy.

Old age and its accompanying disabilities provide an area where non-verbal communication may be needed and art can be used as therapy. Bridie was 82 and severely disabled by paraplegia. She lived in a geriatric hospital and sat in a wheelchair that she could not move by herself; her speech was disordered and she was considered to be depressed. However, when she was invited to join a small art group for an hour and a half a

Figure 6.2 *Circles* Archaic Massive

week, her response was quite startling. She chose to use oil pastels in bright colours and, although she had great difficulty in holding them, she immediately used the only movement that she had, drawing circular shapes which she filled in with diminishing circles to create a solid colour. Bridie was obviously delighted by the colourful effects she achieved (Figure 6.2), and after some weeks she indicated her need to use paint. Although her perseverating movements sometimes tore the wet paper beneath her brush, she continued to enjoy the brilliant colour combinations she could get with this medium. It was most interesting to see that, although she had such limited control, she managed to prevent the colours from being totally merged into a neutral mess by the overpainting. Her enthusiasm drove her to make known her need to paint a house: it seemed to me that she had established the circle and now needed to create a square with the attributes of a home. Her paraplegia created many difficulties and we were both very frustrated at times by failure to control the circular movement of her hand. Eventually she managed a perpendicular line by pushing the brush away from herself, as a child makes its first out-going strokes, and then taught herself to lift her arm at the end of this gesture, blocking the circular perseverating movements. By this means she also managed to achieve diagonals and, finally, the horizontal she needed for the roof. Then she developed a strong and beautiful style of landscape painting in the area of the Massive Transition (Figure 6.3). It seemed that her creative needs had

Figure 6.3 *Landscape* Massive Transition

motivated her to achieve controls that had not been helped by physio-therapy.

In the 1940s, when surgery was commonly used to control flagrant and intractable psychoses, Teresa, a woman in early middle age underwent a modified leucotomy. She had been severely disturbed for a number of years, impulsive and incontinent, living in the seclusion of a side room of a psychiatric hospital, where nothing had been found to help her. At that time it was considered essential that post-leucotomy patients commence a rehabilitation programme as soon as possible after the operation, and when

Figure 6.4 *The little nurse* Archaic Massive

Figure 6.5 *Self portrait* Archaic Massive

Teresa first came to the art room her head was bandaged and she was still suffering from the effects of the anaesthetic. However, she painted a small picture of a ploughed field in dark colours with a small yellow sun with a red spot in it. The painting was made in the style of a Massive Transition, with heavy brush-work and rich purple and blue paint, suggesting that the emotional aspect of the style dominated her intuitive perceptions. However, the painting was surprisingly well organized in view of her muddled state of mind and physical weakness. The following week she was stronger and seemed hopeful and eager to cooperate. She decided to paint a fairground but was disconcerted to find that she could not paint the roundabout as a three-dimensional object with animals at the back as well as the front. She soon gave up the attempt and demanded to be taken back to the ward. In the next session Teresa's style changed to the Archaic Massive and then she found that she could paint anything she liked. The change in style was preceded by her wish to paint a portrait from memory of the young nurse who had dressed her in a clean gown at a time when she was too ill to respond to anyone (Figure 6.4). This painting made in the Archaic Transitional area is a loving tribute to the nurse for the compassion she had shown, and it was followed by several richly painted works in the Archaic Massive style. In some of them outline was altogether abandoned. At first these were full-face, based on a circle, such as the *Self portrait* (Figure 6.5).

Then she made a series of profiles: a fat, complacent, pig-like face (Figure 6.1), thin, witch-like heads, and saintly, idealized people (Figure 6.7). Teresa did not name these faces or seem to regard them as portraits but as works of art. Questioned by another patient, she said, 'I can paint a face any way I want, I can paint it green if I want to,' and proceeded to do so (Figure 6.6). She improved rapidly and her doctor was anxious that she should return to normal life as soon as possible. Unfortunately, as she had been ill for so many years her family had become accustomed to life without her; her place as wife and mother had been taken and her children no longer knew her. She retreated to hospital and painted hideous faces with mad eyes and inverted mouths, like toothless witches. I felt her despair and frustration and asked her what she thought of these paintings. She said she hated them because they were bad and unreal. I felt a need to intervene and suggested that she might have come to a time when she should paint from actual people instead of working from the imagination. We found a patient who was willing to sit for her and Teresa freely painted a likeness that pleased them both (Figure 6.8). A few weeks after this Teresa was finally discharged and remained well, able to learn a trade and earn her living. In view of her long illness and the loss of her family and home it seems wonderful that she was able to make a new life with the help of a relative. Her achievement is more understandable when we consider the symbolic imagery of her work, particularly the portrait of the nurse, in terms of the Circle in the Square. This painting has some linear features and suggests to me that she had integrated the sensuous and emotional parts of her self in terms of a positive experience in the outer world, which she could not achieve in her earlier painting of the roundabout, where the circle was envisaged as an object in space, distanced from the intensity of emotional realization. The cheerful funfair was not the subject to release her powerful emotions and she was frustrated by her failure to represent

Figure 6.6 *Green face* Archaic Massive

external reality. By first making a therapeutic regression in style, Teresa was able to move forward and find the outer world later, in the final portrait from life. Although, on readmission, she seemed on the borderline of madness her paintings were never confused, and the final portrait showed her that she could relate to outer reality. Beneath the appalling symptoms of her illness it seemed that Teresa had maintained a hard core of emotional reality that survived the surgical abuse.

Figure 6.7 *Saint* Archaic Massive

The following example shows one way in which a creative fantasy may develop from a single dream if it is made visible as a drawing or painting.

Martha was a young student when she sought psychiatric help for an anxiety state which she described as totally irrational. Many years afterwards, she told me that at the time she had felt as if the pavement was cracked and that there was no soil beneath to support it. She had been in a car accident and had suffered a bereavement but she told the therapist that

Figure 6.8 *Portrait from life* Massive Transition

Figure 6.9 *Idol* Archaic Massive

she had accepted these experiences as a part of adult life and that they had no bearing on her irrational fears. She did not feel depressed, but was concerned that the formless anxiety might make her lose control and that she would 'escape life, or not get on with it'. Weekly psychotherapy sessions were arranged but Martha said she could not make any use of them at first; only her punctual attendance indicated that she had any hope of help. After some months there was a sudden change; she had a dream about her childhood home in which she discovered a huge granite statue in an adjoining garden. The dream was so clear that Martha felt that she could draw it, and the result surprised her (Figure 6.9). She brought it to her therapist, and when it was propped in his chair she agreed that it bore some likeness to him.

THE CHANGING STYLES OF THE DREAM IMAGE

Martha's therapist did not suggest that she should draw; however, as he had shown interest in this work she made a second drawing, as a result of a formless daydream. The original image then seems to have become part of a continuous, or regular fantasy. Sometimes it seemed almost visible, like a large balloon floating above her head. She said that it had never worried her and, indeed, had kept anxiety at bay. When this phase passed the dream image recurred several more times and her drawings of it seemed to become less solid and distinct. I imagine they changed from the Archaic to the Traditional Massive or the Massive Transition.

About twenty years after these drawings were made Martha told me about them:

I was half inclined to give up coming to therapy when I had that dream. I was dreadfully anxious and tense at the time. I couldn't eat and I wasn't getting any help, as far as I could see. I continued to have terrible dreams and when I woke up alone I was still in them for hours. But this dream was completely different, quite beautiful, warm and everything sparkling as if the rain had stopped and every blade of grass was shining. I could see the granite glittered with bits of crystal. I was afraid to talk about it in case I lost the vividness. I wanted to stay in it but I wanted to tell him [the therapist] as long as he would not say the wrong thing. When he said so calmly that it looked like him and that it was very ugly I was pleased. I had seen that he came into it somehow. I could see a resemblance. Now I think that it would have made an ideal therapist; an impervious, reliable figure, always there. Although I was absolutely sexless at the time, I saw it was a sexual object and drew in the lines of the penis, although I don't remember seeing it in the dream. Afterwards the idol went on in my imagination, it had a sort of tray on legs, or a table for sacrifices. I also saw it as a sort of companion that I could love and despise, particularly when it hovered over my head helplessly. Hovering was what my father did, hovering about, afraid of rows; but I couldn't despise my father, he was too good, always helpful.... The next drawing was made in a notebook only about two inches wide. The idol was scribbled over, swathed in flowers or leaves, like children crawling and slobbering all over it. It looked fat and feminine and it infuriated me, it seemed disgusting like a great fat settee. Isn't that extraordinary – that I wanted to be the only baby to crawl all over it and slobber, but also ... envy. I wanted to be it. To be the one crawled over and messed about. It had also something to do with being a baby with my father. The dream about the bus came later. I didn't draw it. I had the feeling that he [the therapist] could have done more to help but wouldn't. The bus was my life: I was totally unfitted for it. I didn't know how to drive and yet I had to keep at it. There were some suicidal ideas at that time ... considered jumping off. There was a dream about the idol, being in bed ... its head was on the pillow but it was actually kneeling on the floor ... not a success. It brought up the pain of the transference and, of course, of my father not being seducible and me not being able to bear that, even though he was never unkind or laughed at me. All that still saddens me when I think of it ... poor child, poor children. I never dreamt about the idol after that but it cropped up in doodles.... I had intended to make a landscape and then suddenly put in the idol instead of a tree in the distance, in an affectionate way. Of course, that startled rabbit in the foreground might have suggested that there was more to it than that. Then when things went wrong and my marriage was in bits I was doodling and the idol suddenly turned up again, or at least it seemed like that although the drawing of it was quite different, a sort of jester, devil with penis-like tentacles all over it and even on its head, like a jester's cap. I saw immediately how we [her husband and herself] were paralysed and fascinated by all those willies waving about. We were like children faced with a great sexual adult. I simply had to go back and take it to him [the therapist]. It seemed like a horrible bit of dead transference that had come alive again, withering up our life.... Well, would you believe it, I thought I could just take it along and get rid of it. Hand it over. It was so long since I had been in therapy that I'd forgotten it was 'do it yourself'. I was really annoyed when he wouldn't take it. When I got home I felt I had to make one more effort to find out what my unconscious was up to and I made the model. It almost seemed to make itself, except at the back, which I built up until it made a cube. The back was very difficult: I'd never seen it. It was the most marvellous chance that when it dried (and split) off I could look inside for the first time in all those years. Until I could see the idol all round I couldn't see inside it, if you can understand. It had to be black and solid outside but I painted it white and light inside as if the light was on. The outside was a shell, like a signal box with a little man inside; he was small and neat, in a white coat, working the levers. Wasn't that funny? I suppose I had used it over the years to signal different things that I didn't admit – and you might say that it had kept me on the rails if you want to. I can't tell you all the things that I worked out with that idol. That [first] dream was really powerful. It was *real*, and terribly important that it should be real, and yet later it was important that it should not stand in for a real person such as N.... or my therapist, or myself. At first I could not have borne for anyone to have said I made it up, up to the time I made the model, and then I was chuffed that I could make it if I wanted to; but all the same the thing was bigger than skill.... It taught me you can't choose one thing or the other: you have to live with both, whether you like it or not.

Although it is my belief that art as a therapy requires the security of a therapeutic setting, there are instances when exceptional people, or exceptional situations, call up a creative ability that they may not have used since childhood. Benvenuto Cellini, the sculptor is a case in point: as a prisoner deprived of the means to practise sculpture, he was forced to express himself in the only art available to him:

> I cast my eyes around my prison and saw some scraps of rotten brick, with the fragments of which, rubbing one against the other, I composed a paste. Then creeping on all fours, as I was compelled to go, I crawled up to an angle of my dungeon door, and gnawed a splinter from it with my teeth. Having achieved this feat, I waited till the light came on in my prison; that was from 8.30 to 9.30 pm. When it arrived, I began to write, the best I could, on some blank pages of my Bible. He concluded: After this, I recovered strength.　　　　　　　　　　　(Cellini 1927: 246)

In the case of Martha, and that of Mary (below) there was no physical privation which drove them to creative work; their conflict was internal and neither seemed conscious of the degree to which they were suffering until they had created a work of art and give the dissociated feelings a form.

Mary was a successful professional woman, neither a patient nor an artist, but one of those who naturally doodle when their feelings or ideas cannot be expressed otherwise. Although she did not usually show these doodles to anyone, on this occasion she brought me a series of paintings that she had made one evening, when she had decided to paint a tree. I was so interested by the sequence that I asked if I could include them here as examples of the power of creative fantasy.

Mary had noticed a tendency to doodle trees while she was thinking and was curious to know what they might signify. She started to paint an image (Figure 6.10) and soon found herself deeply engrossed, working over her original sketch many times and enlarging the childlike image of a lollypop

Figure 6.10 *Tree* Archaic Massive

Figure 6.11 *Tree/dancer/crucifixion* Massive Transition

Figure 6.12 *Tree/child* Archaic Massive

Figure 6.13 *Hollow tree* Archaic Massive

Figure 6.14 *Snake in the grass* Massive Transition

tree, thickly overpainting it with dark brown and white paint. She added a wide baseline, filling it in to look like a ploughed field covering a strong root that had stretched across the page from right to left. At some stage she widened the trunk of the tree and painted two slender branches that extended beyond the boundary of the circular head of its foliage; this made the treetop look separate from the trunk, as if it were a dark sun, or a disk set behind the body of the tree itself. She finally added some white paint, giving a heavy, corrugated effect to the trunk and the mandala-like head of the foliage. This painting shows typical features of the Archaic Massive style – the strong colour and impression of closeness and convexity.

During the accompanying reverie, the phrase 'a hollow tree' came to her mind. She felt very pleased with this picture, particularly delighted with the strong, rough texture of the bark, which she stroked sensuously when she showed it to me. However, she felt that she had not understood the meaning behind the tree image and she decided to paint again, using a brighter, terracotta brown and black, omitting the white overpainting. She also left out the circle of foliage. As she painted, it occurred that the two branches looked like a dancer's arms, or a crucifixion (Figure 6.11). A little blob of black paint had fallen on the paper, and as Mary played with it she thought of a slug, with its head rearing up against the bole of the tree; she added two little horns but then found the slug rather repulsive. As this painting did not seem to add anything further to her understanding she painted again, this time making the branches shorter and thicker, which she saw as the upraised arms of a very young child (Figure 6.12). In this painting the slug reappeared, it was larger and placed higher up this tree, as if entering the branches in the space where she had imagined the hollow to be. At this moment Mary felt extremely nauseated by the solid mass of the slug, especially when the paint was wet and shiny. Nevertheless, she was determined to know what would happen if the slug got inside the tree, and so painted the subject once again, using the same black and brown, but this time showing the tree as if split open to reveal the slug inside (Figure 6.13). Mary had hoped that the slug would go down to the roots and curl up peacefully, but she suddenly gave way to impulse and added a third branch, effectively pinning the slug between two branches; in doing this she felt that she had changed the fantasy and that it was then on another level.

Mary made one more painting in the sequence, a landscape that was developed in the Transitional Massive style (Figure 6.14). The slug is stretched back and forth across the foreground of a sunny meadow and its head rests rather charmingly on its coils. Mary said that she was surprised to see that the slug had become a harmless grass snake or, possibly, she added, a snake in the grass.

THE VISUAL SYMBOLISM REPRESENTED BY THE STYLES

The first painting struck me by its effect of solidity and weight. The shapes are Archiac, massively overpainted up to an impasto. The style is of intense emotional commitment; the colours, brown and black, are less passionate, more down-to-earth. This strength of form was carried through the following three paintings, although they were not so sensuously overworked. In Figure 6.11 the tree is set back on the horizon line as though the feeling had been somewhat distanced, and in Figure 6.14 this quality of distance has been taken further as recessive space. From this change of style I can understand that her experience of finding herself suddenly working 'on a different level' was in fact a change of mood or attitude from the emotional commitment of Archaic Massive painting to an intuitive perception of the subject expressed in the Massive transition.

Mary's unusual ability to pursue her unconscious fantasy through painting allowed her to reach visual images that we can usually only meet in dreaming sleep. Her first painting provided her with a very powerful image of the circle of self, in the shape of the head of foliage with its lines of force reaching out as branches and trunk of the tree. From this position she was able to imagine a weakness in the attribute – it was a hollow tree. In other words the whole self of the circle could recognize some weakness in its attributes and pursue this in the form of a parasitic slug. Her impulse to halt the slug's descent dramatically altered the tone, or level, of the fantasy and, still without deliberate effort on her part, the style changed and qualified this move. We can see that the slug that menaced the tree in the leafless underworld of the Archaic Massive pictures has surfaced in a pleasant landscape as a harmless grass snake or, perhaps, Mary said, a snake in the grass. This final painting in the sequence is mainly in the Traditional Massive style, although the ambiguity of the snake's nature – harmless or sly – is borne out by the linear quality of its representation: it does not quite fit into the naturalistic scene.

To summarize this chapter, the significance of Archaic Massive art is explored as the visual equivalent of emotional reality. Examples are given of some ways in which emotional realization is discovered and used in visual images that include references to the individuals' particular needs at the time.

Figure 7.1 *Child and swing* Massive Transition

Chapter 7

The Massive Transition
Anthropomorphism and the underworld

In Chapter 5 I identified an area of transition between two basic styles and indicated the symbolic imagery that is implicit in this transitional art. I gave some examples of the consequences of blocks between the Archaic styles and their release through spontaneous work with art materials in therapy. In this chapter another area of transition will be discussed, with particular attention to the effects of a block formed when the two, equally powerful, styles are present in one painting or sculpture. Some features appear in such a case that distinguish this block from any other style and indicate the symbolic meaning that the style presents. Examples of this type of work will be given in a therapeutic context.

THE APPEARANCE

Within the whole area of the Massive Transition some works will be closer to the Archaic, with richness of colour, overpainting or impasto, but showing a diminished scale and multiplicity of attributes given to both main and secondary parts of the work (Figure 7.1). This tends to create a rather impacted effect, with heavy-handedness in the detailing of the attributes and a loss of the lively grace and energetic sweep of the Archaic Massive style. Works that are closer to the Traditional Massive style are more subtle in their effect, colours are less intense, with more spaciousness in design (see Plate 7.4).

Undoubtedly, a most important aspect of this style lies in its sensitivity towards placement. As an Archaic artist comes to add more and more to his picture he makes use of the space that is left at the sides of the central subject, between the base- and skylines. By this means the congestion in the foreground can be relieved. However, once the flat plane of the pictorial surface has been given horizontal lines that indicate the specific attributes of earth and sky, anything that is put between them can look as if it is dangling in mid-air. This difficulty is overcome when a second base-line, or series of base-lines, are added to suggest an ascending background, like shelves on which objects of secondary importance can be arranged. The structural effect of the picture is changed in this way for it is no longer seen as a flat surface; the picture plane is used more like a window-glass through which we can see a view. Then the base-line is moved higher up the page to form a foreground, which has the effect of bending the space above its upper edge at right angles, as if it were the backcloth to a stage. There is still no consistent illusion of recession in this style, but of separate views, placed one above the other and sometimes used like a perpendicular strip cartoon (Figure 7.2).

This use of space is comparable to the use of form in sculptures made in the Massive Transitional style. When we look at one of the colossal lions from Nimrud, carved in 880 BC, now at the British Museum, we can see that the huge blocks of stone were carved in convex, high relief. Although their heads are three-dimensional and their bodies seem to be so when seen from the front or side; at the three-quarter view it is clear that five legs have been carved for each lion because the front and side views have not been conceived as a single form.

POSTURE AND GESTURE

An artist's gestures are affected by the size and scale of his work. However large the overall size, detailed work forces him to move closer to his work and restricts his movements to some extent. The gestures that create the Archaic arts come from the shoulder and arm; the whole body is involved. But as eye and hand focus on smaller areas, wrist and fingers are flexed as well. The transition from Archaic to Traditional art is reflected in a variety of large and small gestures creating the art work. This alteration in scale may give an effect of clumsiness to some painted or sculpted forms (see Plate 7.1).

REVERIE

The style appears to reflect the artist's unconscious preoccupation with integrations of self and other in terms of optimum placement rather than variation in size.

FANTASY

Concerns about placement seem to become conscious in fantasies about related space – the larger and smaller, higher and lower, and so on. These may develop in complex art works or stories about huge Archaic images and their secondary attributes, between ancient gods and human beings, good people and bad little people, evil witches and friendly animals – the whole world of myth and fairy story. There may be a feeling for compromise: the taller may become a little smaller and the smaller a little taller, the bad and good of emotional evaluation may become a little less absolute, or modified to some extent by humour or detachment as the artist comes under the influence of the Traditional aspect of his art.

THE SYMBOLISM

The basic symbol of the Circle in the Square also shows a reduction in scale. Its abstract form was shown in *Buns for everyone* (Figure 3.1) where, to make space for other circles in the square, the central circle is reduced. Space for all means less for all, particularly when every circle has to have its attributes and lines of force – a problem that seemed suddenly evident to the small girl who painted '*Everybody must have their own spider's web*' (Figure 3.4). Rosie's painting of *An orchard* (Figure 4.9) solves this problem by overlapping the circles' edges, but the distinctive self circle may have to survive only as an individual leaf or fruit. In some works the circle seems to be omitted altogether and the mood only concerned with placement – getting everything in. The spider's web painting is an interesting example of the area of Massive Transition which is close to the Archaic, for the young artist used space as sky and groundlines, planting her garden with flowers and people along the bottom line with the foundations of the tall house, yet she

Figure 7.2 *St John the Baptist retiring to the desert*, by Giovanni di Paolo, Massive Transition

Reproduced by permission of the National Gallery, London

finally placed the spider's webs in the remaining areas in the middle of the picture without needing to show how they hung there.

More light may be shed upon the difficult question of the symbolic imagery of this style when we look at the work of a fine artist such as Giovanni di Paolo who painted *St John the Baptist retiring to the desert.* Figure 7.2 is a composite view in which the saint is shown striding out of the city gates and then again, on the stony road to the desert. We are not confused by this; we read the painting as a strip cartoon. Each John the Baptist is the same size and wears the same pink shirt, and carries the same little bundle on a stick. Time, as a sequence of events, has been evaded and distance used as the difference between a stage and its backdrop. Some diagonal paths crossing the cultivated fields act as multiple horizon lines to give an idea of distance without diminishing colour or tone. A use of recessive imagery would have dwarfed the distant Baptist and greyed the pink of his shirt. In di Paolo's painting St John is consistent: the saint remains true to himself at the city gate and in the desert. Nevertheless, the artist's style altogether devalues him to the level of two small details in a landscape. St John is remote, a doll or heroic child in fine clothes – not at all the noble, haggard image we usually see, who wears camel hair and a girdle of skin. The pictorial style distances the artist from his emotions and the suffering of a holy martyr. Giovanni di Paolo shows an overwhelming need for detachment, for it has been projected on to the subject as well as its style. St John reads a book as he marches bravely past the grey, desert rocks.

The area of Massive Transition normally reflects the process of a slow transformation between Archaic and Traditional art. The change is almost imperceptible, proceeding piecemeal as parts of the Archaic or Traditional image become adopted by the second basic style. When this occurs to an Archaic artist, the dominant image is no longer placed centrally and symmetry tends to be given up; profiles replace the full circle of a face, as was seen in the previous chapter when Teresa's dominantly Archaic paintings of imaginary heads became profiles that anticipated a movement towards the Massive Transition before she had made that step in her final painting from life.

THE MASSIVE TRANSITIONAL STYLE

Now I come to describe works that exaggerate the transition in a way that distorts both of the basic, massive styles. I see this as a style in its own right because it shows some typical features, together with those found in the whole transitional area. The scale is reduced and so is the potency of the Archaic colour, for colour is often cool. Line is spasmodic and often crudely imposed upon the form, and space is ambiguous. Images reflect both attributes and representations – like the rocks in di Paolo's painting. In this style we enter the underworld of magical transformation, the conjuring

Plate 1.1 *'Petrol pump'* Archaic Linear

Plate 1.2 *Red head* Archaic Massive

Plate 1.3 *Seascape* Traditional Massive

Plate 1.4 *Bronchoscopy* Traditional Linear

Plate 8.1 *Pink hills* Archaic Massive

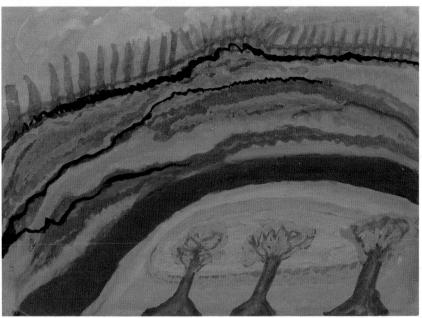

Plate 8.2 *The pale* Archaic Transition

Plate 7.5 *'Lost in the bog'* Massive Transition

Plate 7.6 *Smugglers* Traditional Massive

Plate 7.3 *Pirate priest* Archaic Massive

Plate 7.4 *The cracked chimney* Massive Transition

Plate 7.1 *Stone age picture* Massive Transition

Plate 7.2 *Man and woman* Archaic Massive

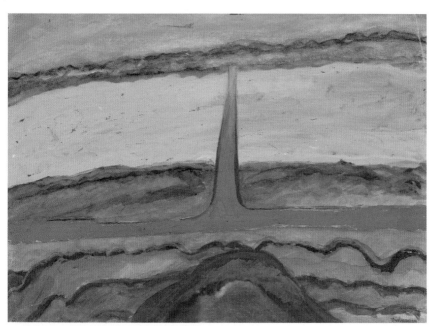

Plate 8.3 *Causeway* Traditional Massive

Plate 8.4 *The river* Traditional Massive

Plate 8.5 *Remembered scene* Traditional Transition

Plate 8.6 *'The man is all right'* Massive Transition

tricks that Pippi needed, the grotesques of the fairground, its mermaid and bearded lady. Fright and humour seem fused in these works, imaging a collision between the inner and outer worlds and, as a result, both are denigrated. The gods are men balancing precariously on stilts, adults are childish and brutal (see Plate 7.3) and children, grotesque adults, animals (Figure 7.1) or gnomes that live underground, energetic and malicious. Nature itself presents a metamorphic shock, for trees have fingers in their branches to scratch and tear. Even the tragedy of death is converted into fear of skeletons and ghosts. The sudden leap of a tiny spider or the scuttling of a cockroach can terrify, and a person can become mentally ill from nameless dread, or even impulsively suicidal.

Giovanni di Paolo seems to maintain a rational attitude, but at the cost of dramatic feeling towards his epic subject. He presents a fairy book version of St John in which only the grotesque rocks at the entrance to the desert suggest metaphysical dangers to be encountered.

THE STYLE IN THERAPY

In this magical, anthropomorphic mood, patients can easily feel hopes or fears about thought transference, about having their mind read by a doctor or therapist, yet may also assume that they will be understood without having to make the effort to communicate. The outer world may seem unpredictable, the inanimate may seem in some way alive. These patients seem very willing to use art as a therapy if they can have the support of a therapist who will represent outer reality while, at the same time acknowledge the validity of the inner world and its threatening images. Change will be clockwise towards the Traditional naturalism of spacial relations or the patient may retreat to the greater emotional certainties of the Archaic Massive style. I saw the latter movement between one painting and the next when Chris suddenly changed his style from the Massive Transition of the *Guitar player* to that of *The witch girl* and its uninhibited emotion (Figures 2.2 and 2.3).

In other cases there would be weeks or months in which a patient might need to work. For instance, Miss Pett, a gentle lady in late middle age, used her delicate mastery of watercolour technique to express and resolve the discrepancy between her inner and outer world by transpositions of foreground and background in her pictures (Figure 7.3). With transparent washes of delicate colour she revealed her need for a child's view of life in an Archaic art that was presented, nevertheless, with a Traditional skill. Her mild, faintly humorous pictures carried her beyond her anxiety and grief, reminding me of G.K. Chesterton's appreciation of the naive point of view, apropos the sculptor Flaxman:

Even foreshortening and perspective he avoided as if there was something grotesque about them, as indeed there is. Nothing could be funnier, properly considered, than the fact that one's father is a pigmy if he stands far enough off. Perspective is the comic element of things.

(Chesterton 1902: 16)

The Massive Transitional style may be used by people who then need to talk about the feelings and recollections it has aroused. Pansy, a small, middle-aged woman was such a person. She arrived at the day hospital art room for the first time, looking very frightened of us, and explained that she found everything alarming. However, she settled down and mixed red and yellow paint with a thick brush, drawing a circle about the size of a teacup in the middle of a large sheet of paper. She packed this circle with crudely painted digits and the hands of a clock at the 10 to 2 position. Above the circular face she painted a dome shape, representing a bell, and two diagonal lines at the base as the legs. Suddenly, she added two pointed ears and these immediately metamorphosed the clock as a grinning elf. We sat contemplating this image for a while and then Pansy remembered the alarm clock that used to waken her for school, and I was able to remind her that she had said that everything 'alarmed' her. Then she spoke about fear of time, of how it tricked her by making her feel that, as an adult she knew no better than a child how to behave. Although the face of the clock

Figure 7.3 *Miss Pett's seaside* Massive Transition

seemed malicious to her it was also impish, and during that session Pansy was able to say that she had often dealt with difficulties by making a joke of it or by trickery and cheating.

Many patients using the Massive Transitional style are too disturbed to talk so rationally. For example, a woman hospitalized with phobic anxiety sat crying and rocking herself as she painted cockroaches, frog-spawn and insects over a large sheet of paper. Later paintings focused her fear on snakes, which became larger in successive paintings until they were huge, convex shapes filling the page in the Archaic Massive style. Then the style became more Traditional; a single snake was shown lying in long grass which sloped, like a bank towards a high horizon. The patient then painted a snake on an island, under a tree. In terms of symbolic imagery the island, as a circle of self now contained the snake, which was no longer projected. After this the transition moved again towards the Traditional Massive style; she painted some naturalistic landscapes in attractive colours, with energetic brush-strokes.

Humour, trickery and magic can have seductive charms that may constitute a pathological defence. Had this patient stayed with the imaginative trick of immuring her snake on a desert island I would have doubted her ability to sustain the balance between inner and outer reality, since it had already broken down. However, her style continued to change, moving further away from the inner, emotional reality of her life while retaining its modifying effect in the warmth and richness shown in the colour and free brush-work of her landscapes.

When chicanery is apparent in a patient's behaviour and not confined to the art work I remain unsure how far this can be beneficial to a patient. It may be a waste of therapeutic time, or a necessary pause in his pursuit of integration. Winnicott (1979: 240) has brought this aspect of therapy into focus with his remarks on the Holding Function and its relation to the risks of dependence, against which such chicanery is an understandable defence. For example, Pippi (Chapter 5) needed me to close my eyes while he set up his elegant but utterly imaginary conjuring tricks. I think that this was an attempt to get my support for his fantasy of omnipotence but I wondered if, by doing so, I was strengthening a delusion, or sharing what both of us realized to be a game.

Massive Transitional art may seem to provide the most obvious and direct route between Archaic and Traditional art – that is, between inner and outer reality. It may also be seen to straddle the primary and secondary mental processes. This art style may also have a particular function in therapy that Freud recognized in art as a whole, as;

> A sanctury during the painful transition from the pleasure principle to the reality principle ... the artist, like the neurotic, had withdrawn from an unsatisfying reality into his world of imagination but, unlike the

> neurotic, he knew how to find his way back and once more get a firm
> foothold in reality.   (1948: 18)

The longer case which concludes this chapter has been chosen to
illustrate characteristics that have already been described as unique to this
transitional area. They provided the patient with visible images of an
underlying attitude which had had a detrimental effect upon his mental and
physical health when it became fixed and habitual. In a remarkable series of
thirteen paintings we can see magical, metamorphic images evolving in an
increasingly naturalistic way, as the form of the artist's basic symbolism is
extended by his intuitive perception of the outer world. The stages of his
recovery are reflected in painting after painting that integrate the nuances
of inner and outer reality with increasing subtlety. I shall discuss the first six
of this series of paintings by the patient John, who was suffering from
pulmonary tuberculosis. Some aspects of his work have already been
discussed elsewhere (Simon 1970).

John came from Ireland as a casual labourer during the 1940s but soon
became incapacitated by a disease which, at that time was mainly treated by
surgery or bedrest. He was prescribed strict bedrest, but was a very intractable patient, unable or unwilling to lie still in the ward all day. When I was
asked to see him his bed had been moved outside and he was by himself on
a concrete step heading to the small hospital garden where two other
patients lived in open chalets. His only protection from the weather was a
narrow glass roof, a tarpaulin blind that could be pulled down at the open
side of his bed and a red rubber sheet to spread over the bedcovers if it
rained or snowed. Later he acquired a bedside locker and a visitor's chair.
Bedrest was difficult enough to achieve in London when there were air
raids day and night; John had apparently disturbed the other patients, and
for this reason had been put outside the ward.

John was very thin and tense, continually on the move in his bed, and his
habitually anxious expression contradicted his flow of facetious chatter. He
seemed to adopt the role of the stage Irishman and described his present
existence as a joke that was totally unreal, not to be taken seriously for a
moment. He said that he could see stars and anti-aircraft fire above his
head at night. He was quite willing for me to leave him some art materials,
cheerfully assuring me that he would be unable to use them as he was only
a caveman. I suggested that if he liked to express himself as a caveman he
might enjoy painting, and when I next visited him he showed me a rough
brush drawing representing a flat rock, as if seen from above, shaped at the
corners and covered with strange drawings of men and animals (Plate 7.1).
Each figure held something; one held a club, another appeared to lift a lid
or trap over a small animal. Some of the men had distorted heads like
animals, one a beak-like head or head-dress. The painting, in the Massive

Transitional style, looks as if it had been made in an unthinking, dream-like state of reverie. However, some verbal fantasy developed, for John pointed out a line of small creatures enclosed in odd shapes placed, as it were, on the side elevation of the stone. He told me that these were stones that had been cracked open to show 'the fossils within'. I wondered if these images reflected his feeling of being fossilized, or trapped by illness, but John was obviously unwilling or unable to talk about his feelings. He preferred to spin yarns about practical jokes in which either his medicine or the box containing his infectious saliva had spilt. He said he had shown his painting to me to prove that he was no artist, but when I left him he said that I might find another picture if I came again.

On my next visit John showed me a sketch of two large figures (Plate 7.2). These figures had been drawn in the Archaic Massive style in pencil and then filled in roughly with washes of black and pink paint. By watering down the thick gouache I had provided, and only using two colours, he had made a strange and striking work. However, he was so frustrated by the modelling on the faces that he had scribbled moustaches and beards on both. It seemed to me that this failure might cause him to give up painting altogether, but instead he asked me to show him how to make faces look round. He rapidly drew some faces in outline and I gave a brief demonstration to show how the addition of a couple of tones in opaque paint could create a three-dimensional effect. He later adopted the technique of overpainting to develop his work generally and could continue to work on one painting for weeks on end. Although John had betrayed an interest in art by asking for this advice he rarely spoke about his work, and his manner continued to fend off any serious discussion. I thought that the figure on the left looked like John himself and that the right-hand one might be a woman. The style indicates a degree of emotional involvement with painting that John did not show in any other way.

The next time I visited John he had another painting to show me (Plate 7.3). Parts of this painting had been overworked several times. The sketchiness of his first pictures was now replaced by a well-developed painting of figures in a landscape. It looked as if it had been painted at different times, and his mood had varied, for it showed evidence of three different styles – Archaic Linear in the left-hand figure, Archaic Massive in the central figure and the Massive Transition in the stage and background. This is an extraordinary painting that seems to refer to an atavistic world. John's defensive chatter continued, and, although he seemed to ignore the painting, he allowed me to take it up and study it. By this time I felt that we had come to a precarious agreement: he would allow me to contemplate the paintings as much as I liked if I did not question him or say anything that he did not ask for. My attention was at first caught by the strange, yellow figure on the left. It had been drawn in pencil, then painted and finally outlined with black paint. This gave it a flat, linear effect. I saw that this figure had originally been drawn down to the bottom of the page, but as the foreground had been widened it now coloured the lower part of the figure to some extent. Overpainting had not totally obscured the original idea and consequently gave the impression that the figure's skirt was half buried in sandy soil, or that the figure was rising up from the ground like Ceres the corn goddess.

It seemed to wear a head-dress or crown that extended upwards in several layers and gave it equal height to that of the second figure. The whole effect of the 'goddess' is of weakness and unreality, for it is flat, paper-thin and seems to have a dazed, withdrawn expression, as if the intense, hypnotic gaze of the central figure had overwhelmed it. I wondered if the goddess was a symbolic image of John's inability to deal realistically with his illness and its threat to his life. This might be one part of the symbol's meaning and, if it were so, might explain why the figure was not worked up with the same richness of imagination as had been given to the central image. The other figure, painted in the Archaic Linear style, seemed to have been created from sensuous experience alone, while the central image, with its Massive overpainting shows a style that is further round the circle of styles. This image seems to express conflicting emotions for, in spite of representational details such as the pipe and hat, the image, with its long robe and hypnotic stare remains an Archaic picture of John's inner world. Its wide, Archaic skirts spread along the lower edge of the painting, and seem almost within touching distance of the viewer – an androgynous image of violent power, I thought.

The picture as a whole might be imagined to have come to portray conflict between the power of death and the weakness of a life that is hypnotized by death. Originally the figures were linked, hand in hand and, although John had half painted out this line, he had left traces of the earlier position as if he had not been quite sure where he wanted the arms to be.

It was possible that the basket of fire that swung from the left arm in the original drawing had suggested to John that he might paint the figure as a priest, for the long robe had been painted black like a cassock. Later he had added the lines of paint that made a skeleton, and then this, in turn, had been covered with a wash of green paint. Transformations had taken place on the head also, a hat had been added – a large, cowboy-type hat, outlined or haloed with yellow paint and having a diagonal cross in yellow paint on it. This reminded me of the pirate's skull and crossbones. At one stage the figure had been given a huge pipe, which seemed to be an effort to degrade the image with childish mockery.

The changing styles in this picture give important clues to its therapeutic meaning. Unconscious symbolism has been developed during the hours spent in its creation. John first drew the figures with pencil and a painted outline, then he coloured and recoloured them. In many places the overpainting is incomplete and the development of the fantasy is seen rather like a photograph in which several exposures of the subject have been imposed. The original Archaic Linear drawing contributes to the symbolism in several parts of the work, while the central figure is worked over in a way that transforms it into the Archaic Massive style. The background is painted as a Massive Transition 'stage and backdrop'. In a single painting John shows a clockwise movement in the circle of styles, ending with Massive green overpainting. In terms of mood this reads as a partial extension of sensuous dominance to emotions that had been aroused by the central image, together with a certain degree of detachment through the setting of a stage and backdrop. We can see the original reverie taken up by active fantasies that draw it towards rational associations and emotional response. The painting reflects a development that might be variously described: as a shift from primary process thinking to secondary elaborations, or from Archaic to primitive art or even from the figuration of a preschool child to that of an older one.

I was particularly encouraged by John's new ability to paint, to work on his picture with care and attention that enriched his power of creative initiative as well as the symbolic meaning it could have for him in terms of primordial fears. It seemed that these were becoming linked with childhood defences – in the cowboy hat and the pipe. In the background painting I felt that John was beginning to envisage the necessity of giving his fears their rightful place in the natural world where some distancing might be possible, indicated by the delicate painting of the snowy sky.

John's next painting is a landscape without figures (Plate 7.4). It is painted with transparent washes in the Massive Transitional style, using the convention of multiple horizons on which trees and an amorphous building have been set back from the central feature; this appears to be a rather decrepit mill and engine house. In this painting the effect of distance is not consistent; however, it gives a superficial impression of space, particularly at the right side of the chimney. The sky on the left is overcast by cloud from which a small red sun appears. The main feature of the painting is not brought down to the lower edge of the paper, as in Plates 7.2 and 7.3, but to the upper edge of the base-line, or 'stage', which might represent a pond. The building and its tall chimney abut each other, set at an angle which gives the impression of mutual support. This building, with its pointed roof is typical of houses drawn in the Massive Transitional style; a window in the centre of a facade gives the effect of a face. In this case there are no windows in the upper part and the 'house-face' seems without eyes, yet somehow giving me the impression that it revealed fear and woe. The tall chimney stack is shown in X-ray. We see smoke rising up and coming out of a hole as well as from the top.

When John handed me the painting he drew my attention to the chimney that, he said, was cracked and leaking, and I was struck by the intensely malicious tone he used to say this. It gave me a strong impression that John, as well as I, saw an anthropomorphic effect in the whole picture and that he was using mockery and rejection against the chimney as an image in the inner world. Above, the pale eye-like sun seems to stare anxiously at the black pall of smoke. The actual composition of the picture is harmoniously organized. In terms of the basic circle, the smoke curves round the central area behind the main buildings and links with the other details of the landscape. Whatever, or whoever, the chimney stands for, it has some space about it and to that space John had added visual re-collections of the outer world. In this painting he seems to have achieved some quality of distancing and is seeing in his mind's eye with some detachment. This attitude towards his work could be essential if he was to continue and not be frightened by the strange images that were appearing.

Of course these ideas were my own and kept to myself. Similarly, John kept to himself all the fantasies and memories that had contributed to his picture and in no way allowed me to ask him anything about the subject or content. I would have liked to tell him that it reminded me of William Blake's description of a similar anthropomorphic fantasy that he termed a double vision: 'With my inward eye 'tis an old man grey, with my outward, a thistle across my way' (Blake 1939: 322). After arguing with the 'old man', Blake had struck him down, in the same spirit, it seemed to me, as John's when he spoke of the chimney that was cracked and leaking.

John's next painting did, in fact, develop an effect of three-dimensional recession (Plate 7.5). Two figures are set back in a misty landscape in pearly colour/tones. The foreground is rather dark and leads consistently to a lighter background, suggesting twilight. The figures seem to stand clumsily, near the foreground; the legs of the one on the left are hidden below the knee but the other figure seems to lurch or stagger. Behind him, on the right of the painting stands a small dog whose down-turned tail and large eye give it an expression of fear. The figures are mainly painted white; only the legs of the central figure are coloured; both figures wear strange head-dresses like bonnets that meet under the chin. Their faces have fright-ened expressions, with open months. The whole atmosphere is of super-natural and ghostly apprehension.

John told me that he had great difficulty in getting the figures apart. He did not want them to seem to hold hands and asked me for advice (which he did not use); he told me that the picture had a title 'Two men lost in a bog', and added that 'the wee dog is scared to death'. This painting was the first since the original 'caveman' painting in which John had shown a figure with legs. To my mind the long skirts in Plates 7.2 and 7.3 seemed to encumber or even to immobilize the wearer, transforming the image of a living person into some sort of mythical being. As we sat contemplating this work I realised that John was quiet and that it was the first time that he had been able to give up his defensive chatter. At the end of the session, as I moved to the door behind him, he said, off-handedly, as if it had no relevance to the painting, 'My father died of TB you know.'

On my next visit John was in high spirits but sent me away as, he said, he was working on an idea for a painting of smugglers and it was not finished yet. As far as I knew, this was the first time that he had planned a picture in advance, and it suggested to me that he was turning more and more to the use of art as an image of the outer world that could help him to restore equilibrium between his inner reality and the frightening circumstances of his actual life. It seemed that he might become sufficiently absorbed in creative work to benefit both mentally and physically. I was not at all prepared for the mood I had to meet when I visited him on the following week. John was very angry, inarticulate and distressed; he told me very definitely that I was to take the art materials away as he would not be using them again. He spoke so finally that I felt concerned and told him something to the effect that I would be sorry if he broke off the interest in art that we had shared, and an original way of working that had developed so consistently. At last he allowed me to draw out the chair and sit with him. Then I could ask if he had completed the painting of the smugglers. He indicated that it was lying on the ground on the concrete under his bed and that I could get it out. He asked if I could recognize the figure on the left (Plate 7.6). He said it was like his doctor and I had to explain to him that I had never seen the man. I wondered if John's distress was caused by the doctor, for it was common for medical or nursing staff to joke about a patient's art work or even damage it in fun as they had no idea how important it could be for its creator.

When John seemed a little calmer I asked him if he considered that the painting was finished, but he only said it was no good. I asked him if this was due to some technical difficulty that I could help with, and he eventually pointed to the pink weapon in the hand of the figure on the left, whom he said was a guarda. This was wrong, he said, because it seemed stuck to his trousers. I seized on this problem and suggested that he could change the effect by painting the trousers a darker colour, but John mixed some pale grey and used it to outline the gun.

In this painting we see once again a remarkable change in style. The Massive Transition has mainly given way to the naturalism of the Traditional Massive style. The figures are set right back in the picture, crowded up against the top, distanced from the spectator by an expanse of water. They are fully representational, having the proportions of adult men, in comparison with the clumsy, childish figures of the previous painting. They enact the drama in their posture and gesture – the guarda swaggers with his rifle and gun ready, standing with his legs wide apart, his face a healthy red, while the smugglers are pale and anxious, bent under the weight of a long, coffin-like box or boat that they carry. This strange object is decorated with mysterious designs. I was filled with curiosity that John would not, or could not relieve. His manner forbad any questioning and I was not at all sure that he knew what the picture was about. To me the latent content seemed to speak of a threat to life in a very realistic way. The central figure had a death-like face and made me think of John's father, who had died from tuberculosis. The right-hand figure reminded me of John himself, and I noticed that his left hand, which holds a pink knife or dagger, had been repainted several times, each alteration replacing the arm in a lower position, perhaps as a means of concealing the knife from the guarda or giving up his defence.

We have here an example of the special sort of difficulty we meet when a patient cannot or will not talk about his pictorial work. We might imagine that Archaic art contains most of the fantasy accompanying it in the form of an unconscious reverie and that often little of this could be put into words. However, when the style of a work is Traditional and the fantasy has drawn on perceptual images, it seems that a great deal of conscious thought and feeling has gone into its making. Should we try to persuade a patient to talk for his own good or for our own benefit? Does his silence show a lack of trust or, a magical delusion of thought transference? Is it a lack of the right words, or a lack of need to talk to the therapist about the ideas and feelings that have been aroused? Jung seems quite sure that

> a mere execution of the pictures is not all that is required. It is necessary to have an intellectual and emotional understanding of them; they must be consciously integrated, made intelligible and morally assimilated. We must subject them to a process of interpretation.   (Jung 1949: 82–3)

However, on the previous page he speaks of 'that bias which makes us all put the ego in the centre of our lives – and this bias comes from the over-valuation of consciousness.'

I myself have come to feel that consciousness arises during the creative activity of painting but that this is not necessarily something that can be put into words, and it does not necessarily have less integrative force if it is not put into words. Perhaps sometimes we are so much aware of the bad effects of repression that we mistrust anything that is not verbalized in therapeutic work.

John's emotional outburst could have arisen from many sources: he now had a great deal to try him that he had previously ignored by his attitude of disengagement. Now that he had become interested in creating pictures he had given up this invulnerability and may have gained a critical insight into the content of his fantasy, that had forced it beyond the dissociated freedom of creative play. The quality of the overpainting indicated an intense commitment to the creative images, and John might have become enraged on the smuggler's behalf against a guarda who had all the guns. The captives might reflect his own helplessness or even force him to recognize that his illicit behaviour, in crazy antics and practical jokes in the ward, had jeopardised the treasure of his life. However, such speculations about the content lead us beyond the scope of this book.

In the painting style we see that the Massive Transition has approached the Traditional Massive style. The use of distance is still without full recession – the land seems to slope up and the figures do not recede in space, for we can see all the details of their appearance.

It seems that John is assessing life in accord with the complexity of the outer world. The basic symbolism seems dominated by a cruciform arrangement rather than a circle in a square. The painting has a lopsided look, as if it were only partially integrated or, in some way, incomplete.

In summary, the Massive Transition develops as a form of integration in the area between the Archaic and Traditional styles. Art works in this area reflect various degrees in which subjective, emotional states can be related to impartial perceptions of external reality. Such relations have a modifying effect upon both inner and outer images of the self. This area of transition can become concerned with images of altruism, such as the basic abstract symbolic image of the three-year-old who painted *Buns for everyone* (Figure 3.1). Developed in the Massive Transitional form, the style can recur throughout life and appears in the art of old and handicapped patients, such as Bridie (Figure 6.3).

During the process of adjustment between the demands of inner and outer reality, conflicts arise that may become habitual. These create a recognizable style and associated content. The main effect is anthropo-morphic, for the inner, subjective reality of the circle and its attributes imposes upon the outer, objective world of representational appearances an effect that is epitomized by the grotesque distortions and macabre humour of fairground and folk-tale. John, whose paintings have been discussed at length in this chapter, made a therapeutic regression from the area of Massive Transition to the Archaic Massive style. Later, like Teresa (Figure 6.8), he returned to the Massive Transition in paintings that show typical features of stage and backdrop, and atavistic, anthropomorphic images. Then his work moved on in style to include many representational effects. All the paintings I show here were made one after another, without a break. They show the creative impetus in this remarkable man.

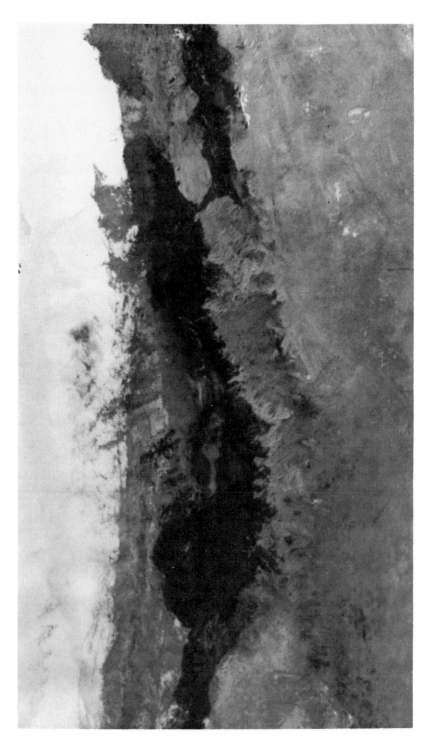

Figure 8.1 *Mrs Bird's landscape* Traditional Massive

Chapter 8

The Traditional Massive style
Intuitive perceptions of space and time

The preceding chapters have been concerned with images that express the dominance of our inner world of sensuous and emotional reality. In Chapter 7 we could see that this subjective view was modified when the individual turned to the external world, and now I will discuss the art that is created by this change of attitude and often seems to introduce it. I will indicate the advantages of this change and also the difficulties that can arise when the world of imagination is limited by our dependence upon the objective values that are presented by our senses and the assumptions that arise from them.

THE APPEARANCE

Traditional art presents a distant view, an image of art that is given a certain detachment, as an opportunity to look at life in a general way that Winnicott describes as shared reality. This view has been popular since Renaissance times for it offers the pleasure of sharing part of our lives with others, or at least the impression that we can see what the artist has seen, as it was. In fact this art is as selective as any other, but its value lies in a dedication to the relativity of visual experience. The artist is fascinated by chiaroscuro and the minutiae of effects that give an illusion of space and light. These overweigh his concern with colour and solid mass which are both modified by the complexities of spatial relation. Distance is suggested by the diminished size of the object represented, but also in the modification of its colour/tone. Consequently, everything that is presented is conditional, depending upon everything else and affecting everything in return.

This sensibility to spatial relation is particularly obvious in sculpture of the Traditional Massive style. The works present three-dimensional images as volumes affected by space. We are not given the clear outline that would suggest a limiting boundary to the form, like the fixed line of a horizon in the 'flat earth' sense, but are visually stimulated to move ourselves or our eyes by the broken or fluid planes that suggest forms continuing beyond our sight. The sculptor is aware that back and front must relate, and this concern leads him to reduce the finality of any fixed view. Sculptors such as Giacometti and painters like Rembrandt extend our experience of forms in space for the forms are broken into fragments of light and shade that divert our attention from any fixed point; our eyes are kept on the move, and the whole surface seems to shimmer like leaves stirring on a tree. Large areas are broken up, continually lost and found again. This broken texture erodes the outline with light and shade, distancing us emotionally and sensuously from the works; we are not seduced by smooth convex shapes and clearly founded forms but must stand back and look with an unfocused gaze, until the whole figure seems to draw itself together and integrate with its surrounding space.

POSTURE AND GESTURE

Traditional Massive art is created by a psychophysical response to stimuli that arises from perceptions of the outer world. These perceptions are of a special kind, being concerned with the subtleties of light and space. The artist's hand hovers tentatively over his work with short brush-strokes: when modelling he uses little pieces of clay. Colours tend to be mixed on a palette and then adjusted further by overworking with broken lines or dots. His hand moves continually beyond the area of focus so that no part of the work is completed before another. By comparison with the Archaic artist, his movements and posture seem restricted.

REVERIE AND FANTASY

In this style recession appears to be the particular quality of the uncon-scious compulsion to integrate self and other. Unconsciously, the basic circle in the square is visualized as a tunnel or spiral; in this shape the colour/tones may remain abstract, or the fantasy develops from spacial apperception peopling it with representations that are related in space. In the art of the cinquecento, this was *sfumato* (soft blending of light and shade).

> *Sfumato* is the unity of people with nature; when it is achieved this unity expresses a profound combination or sympathy between human and cosmic nature; which only suggests the internal structure of form through a tight series of light, quick and intangible brush-strokes.
>
> (Argan 1968)

Landscapes and seascapes present ideal subjects. The pictorial rendering of space as volume and atmosphere, lightness and darkness, mistiness, and so on affects all images within it, and they, in turn, affect the other parts of the picture. Fantasy in this style is closely modelled on things seen and re-collected from outer reality, drawing intuitively upon aspects that obliquely refer to spiritual or emotional meanings. The art of the Traditional Massive painter induces emotion recollected in tranquillity – whether he works from the immediate impact of things seen or imagined.

THE SYMBOLISM OF THE STYLE

The vista is a perfect image of detachment from the immediacy of emotional reality and the twilight world of metamorphosis. In his prevailing mood the Traditional Massive artist views the Archaic world as irrational, tumultuous and claustrophobic. He is drawn to the temperate regions of recollection and nostalgia or the immediacy of perceptual reality. His need to give precise spatial relation to everything he paints has a hidden metaphysical meaning – in Argan's words, 'the unity of people with nature'. This is almost the opposite of the previous style, in which the grotesque and strange aspects of nature demanded integration. The Traditional Massive artist looks coolly at everything under the sun, and gives everything equal value in appearance. This has the effect of levelling the value of everything and equalizing the significence of all that he sculpts, paints and draws. Fashioned by light and shade, at a distance the human figure is presented as a few brush-strokes, barely distinguishable from a tree or a rock.

Although Traditional painters may acquire skills and philosophies about their art, the style can arise spontaneously, without any deliberate effort to recollect an inspiring view. For example, Mrs Bird (designated Mrs B, in Hamilton and Simon 1980) aged 92 had been hospitalized for five years with senile dementia. She had sat in the ward all day, with closed eyes, and seemed totally confused and upset when she was introduced to the art room. She did not remember me from one week to the next or seem to understand why she was given art materials. At first she tried to smoke the pastel I gave her like a cigarette, but when I called her attention to the accidental marks she had made by banging it on the paper like a drum she drew a few horizontal lines. After that, she chose colours that suggested landscape – blue placed at the top of the page and so on (Figure 8.1). When she had finished an area of colour to her satisfaction she would put down her brush carefully. She worked in horizontal masses that were blended together in a way that suggested three-dimensional space. I was fascinated to see how she did this, as she only used one colour at a time. Her choice of colour/tone was impeccable in giving the effect of landscape, each in a difficult range of harmonious colour/tones (McCourt *et al.* 1984: 101–4). A landscape might be made in light tints, say pinks and pale blue, or in strong tones of brilliant blue and gold. If the colours seemed to abut in a flat, two-dimensional way and threaten the continuity of the spacial relation, Mrs Bird would overwork the edges until they gave the impression of continuous recession. Although she was considered disorientated in space and time, it seemed that she could realize these qualities visually. Mrs Bird could only score 7 out of 36 points in the Royal College mental test and, according to her family, had not painted before. As I wondered if I might be projecting an idea of landscape upon work that she might see differently, I asked Mrs Bird if she could tell me something about one of her paintings. She replied, 'I just could not tell you … it's quite early … where we can go for our reasonable life.… The pink is very nice and we'll have more room for the.… The clouds are too high but the other blue is top-heavy. The white is nice and clean.' From these remarks it is clear that Mrs Bird was not visually confused by her painting but saw it as a landscape. By describing it as a place for reasonable life she indicated her moderate views.

This is one example of my experience that visual symbolism is more significant than verbal thought to people who can give it an image, whether this is in a Traditional or Archaic style. As another example, a middle-aged man hospitalized with aphasia and alexia was a devoted painter in the Traditional Massive style. He worked from sight, painting anything he saw in the ward. His work had a dynamic roughness of texture that implied some influence from the Massive Transition, giving his images a tactile quality that brought them closer in feeling than the more usual detachment shown in this art style. His efforts to speak were very frustrating and he seemed to escape into non-verbal communication by painting. One day I happened to have with me a painting by the artist of Plate 1.4. It was an abstract representation of a sensation of pain, made in the Traditional Linear style. To my astonishment, the patient, who normally could not complete a sentence, was able to use a sequence of words as he studied this work. He said, 'I remember standing on a mountain – a hill – and the boy threw a stone at my head.'

The Traditional Massive artist seems to draw on an endless store of visual recollections. At one time I worked with a young man who was suffering from a protracted disease that confined him to bed. He used a sketch book as a means of travelling in imagination, drawing with a thick pencil a continuous landscape that extended either side of each page, which he used like the folds of a Japanese screen. Page after page the scene continued smoothly, from countryside to town, through suburbs, over bridges, rail-tracks and rivers, past factories and goods yards. Everything was indicated in space and light, set against a distant range of hills. The panorama started with a drawing of his bed, as seen from his chest, showing his lower arm and hand and the view out of the window. Then his imagination took flight; his attitude to objects was quite impartial, he drew a rose garden and a rubbish tip with equal enjoyment of their visual effect.

As I see it, the obvious benefit of the Traditional Massive style for the artist lies in its power to evoke familiar experiences of shared reality. The self, as a part of this shared reality, is at home in a world that limits individual experiences and passions to the boundary of the square – the limits of objective reality. The circle of self is concealed within the imagery of natural phenomena, unconsciously designing its harmonious effect. Traditional Massive artists use the integrating effect of the circle in a square without necessarily understanding the symbolic meaning. Artists such as Gainsborough composed their work in this way. For example, his painting of *Mr and Mrs Andrews* (Figure 8.2), shown seated in their extensive estate, delights us as much by its harmonious composition as by the charm of its subject matter. Although the underlying arrangement of the design remains hidden, and we are not forced to notice the elegant proportions of circle to square, we can search out and enjoy the ease with which the artist has assembled it. Reading clockwise from the curve of foliage at the top of the painting, the eye is coaxed down through the changing colour/tones of the clouds to the far edge of the haycocks and then the circle is carried by tufts of grass and the curve of Mrs Andrews' skirt that sweeps around to meet the curve of her husband's arm. The tree trunk is conveniently bulged on the left side to carry the eye up to the shadow of the overhanging branch. The hidden circle ensures that the figures are comfortably held in the middle distance.

The intuitive sense of relation that we see in Traditional Massive art can be found in individuals who have never considered themselves to be artistic. Such an individual may live satisfactorily throughout a long life in terms of his intuitive relation to others until perhaps, at last, body and mind

Figure 8.2 *Mr and Mrs Andrews,* by Thomas Gainsborough, Traditional Massive

unite to assert the essential need to claim the fundamental egocentricity of Archaic realities, for

> Naught loves another as itself
> Nor venerates another so,
> Nor is it possible to Thought
> A greater than itself to know. (Blake 1939)

Miss Rink was one who seemed to have lived in harmony with others for most of her life. Her character was set as a strong and benign authority, and at 93 she was living in a private residence for old people. Although the oldest inhabitant, she was greatly admired and could always be depended upon by staff and residents to maintain rigorous standards of behaviour – the good manners in which there is no place for outbursts of emotion. In such an habitual attitude her feelings about approaching death would be rational, or even prosaic. The professed aim was for death to be no trouble for anyone. When we first met, Miss Rink graciously accepted art materials and immediately used blue chalk to make some weak spirals across the page from left to right, almost as if she was handwriting. She worked over part of this scrawl with smaller spirals and spoke of their likeness to clouds. She said that she would join the weekly art group as she 'found the experience very entertaining'. Although it seemed that her attitude was detached and her work was to be abstract, during the following weeks she added paint to her picture, slowly transforming it into a naturalistic sea-scape. She added a number of details – seagulls, a lighthouse and a light-ship, a destroyer and a marker buoy (Plate 1.3). These images are set in the middle distance. When the painting seemed finished Miss Rink overpainted some distant cliffs to represent a huge wreck, and then added curving lines to the foreground, which she explained as the passage of a torpedo underneath the water that was heading for the sinking ship. The whole scene is delicately set out with tentative brush-strokes that obscure its emotional impact. Up to this point Miss Rink had painted without help, but now she asked me for a little advice. She had originally painted a natural-istic sun on the left side of her picture, using horizontal strokes of yellow and white as if the sun was seen through clouds. Now she had come to feel that this was unsatisfactory, and in trying to alter it she feared that the sun had become too big. I told her that in a painting, the sun, or anything else can be any size the artist wants it to be. She was easily reassured, saying 'Then I shall make it bigger!' – which she did, adding heavy rays to an Archaic Massive disk. Miss Rink was very pleased with the effect that she had created, but she did not carry out her intention to make another painting for, unexpectedly, she became very weak and died a few weeks later.

In a single painting Miss Rink showed her need to integrate her intuitive perceptive view of life with a deeper understanding of its eventual destruction. At first this seems to have been presented as a balanced view – the destroyer and red marker buoy balanced by the lighthouse and lightship. However, when the painting seemed finished she added further images of destruction that were not so perfectly integrated within the whole scene; the disproportionate wreck and the strong blue direction lines of the torpedo. Stronger feelings were indicated that seemed to call up the need of the symbolic image of the whole self-circle, the Archaic sun. I hope that this emotional strength in her painting sustained her against physical weakness that otherwise might have depressed her final days (Simon 1981).

DEPRESSION

Anyone whose life forces them to live with a terminal state, or permanent handicap is likely to be affected by bouts of depression. This type of depression is different in quality from that described as 'agitated depression' that is associated with the Massive Transitional style (Chapter 7).

Winnicott (1988: 72) likens the depressed mood that is not psychotic to a fog or mist that blankets the inner self when the patient is threatened by loss of integration. This effect can be seen in the Traditional Massive style when a naturalistic painting fails to 'come together' and looks muddled. Although the background may be shown in recession, the foreground falls away in a precipitous drop. Colour/tone is neutral and the tentative brush-work becomes a fuzzy overpainting that blurs rather than reveals the three-dimensional effects. In some cases this mood becomes habitual and the patient seems unwilling or unable to interest himself in anything. Even if he is initially attracted to the idea of creative art, his apathy and loss of self-esteem put many obstacles in the way. He finds colours too strong and clay too pliable; he fears to impose anything upon the 'perfect' unbroken surface of canvas or paper. He suffers silently behind a blank mask of hopelessness. Yet art as therapy can offer the opportunity to recover the power of choice. It can be an innocuous dialogue between the manifest material in hand and the depressed creative drive.

A loss of colour and form in the Traditional Massive style indicates a loss of this aspect of the integrating symbol – the circle in a square. The inner world seems overwhelmed by impingements from external reality that lack the order and structure that an intuitive sense of self-identity can give. The loss of spacial relation in his art reflects the artist's loss of his inner space and distancing that is the structure of his habitual attitude of detachment. Although space may continue to be represented as distance, it is not maintained in the foreground where the effect of closeness fails and the bottom part of the work appears as a precipitous drop.

A person's depression may be so intense that he needs to be cared for until he recovers his ability to care for himself. He may need help to get to therapy and to get brush to paper. For example, when Edward, a sensitive artist, was faced with a disabling disease, he became increasingly depressed and inert. At our first meeting he seemed physically weak and his speech was slow and hesitant. He was not withdrawn but, in view of his age, a question was raised about the possibility of dementia. His art had always been Traditional Massive in style, but he had given up painting, and the few drawings he did make were fuzzy and confusing. He could no longer enjoy painting from sight or imagination although he remained sensitive to the effects of landscape and flowers. Short, intensive therapy was offered in a residential setting and he agreed to attend regularly. Within two weeks of individual work with the therapist he had recovered his creative initiative. In the therapeutic setting Edward was able to express his natural grief about his infirmity, which I have called 'self pity' and described elsewhere as 'bereavement' (Simon 1981). Then his art work became stronger in composition, with brighter colours and livelier brush-work. Edward sought out attractive subjects and his physical tone improved. He returned to his previous personality, a kind teacher and responsive friend.

The fact that the Traditional Massive style reflects an attitude that can be overwhelmed by depression, does not, of course, mean that artists have a particular responsiveness to light and space because they are depressives. Impressionist art is shaped by intuitive perceptions of external reality, but its artists cannot be assumed to be depressed.

Brief examples such as Edward's can seem like fairy tales. For this reason I shall present two longer ones, showing the painful efforts that are needed when a patient's previous life has not been at all as tranquil and secure as Edward's had been.

In Chapter 7 I discussed some paintings by John, whose pulmonary tuberculosis had introduced him to art as therapy. The first six of thirteen paintings he made (Plates 7.1 to 7.6) were discussed in terms of conflict between Archaic, magical thinking and the realization and acceptance of external reality that is implicit in the Traditional Massive style. Now I will present the rest of John's paintings in light of his use of external reality as a defence against the magical effects of the inner world that is imaged in Massive Transitional terms. John had made a therapeutic regression from the Massive Transitional style to the Archaic Massive. From then on the paintings form an unbroken sequence of clockwise development until broken off at the time when he painted the smugglers (Plate 7.6). This painting showed a lack of consistent recession and a precipitous drop in the foreground that is seen in many works by depressed people who paint in this style. At this critical time, when John seemed to be viewing life more realistically he became too angry to finish this painting.

I had expected that John was too deeply committed to painting to give up altogether, but I was agreeably surprised to find that he had already begun again when next I visited him. He showed me a painting of pink and brown hills that were set back from a wide foreground (Plate 8.1). His style had returned to the Massive Transition and convex form dominated over recessive space, indicating that his emotional concern was in conflict with his need for detachment. The work had not been overpainted, but John had used a technique that I had not seen him use before: he had washed out and re-worked the original painting, and traces of this work showed that the fore-ground had contained huge trees and that there had been a large bird in the sky: the work had originally been made in the Archaic Massive style.

John was surly, but did not seem to be at all concerned by his return to an Archaic style. Although he had used Traditional naturalism in the smugglers painting, he did not appear to prefer it to the Archaic or try to sustain it, as most amateur artists would. The next paintings showed a spontaneous development of the Massive Transition: the pearly colours and dwarfed forms (Plates 8.2, 8.3 and 8.4) are reminiscent of the bog painting (Plate 7.5). However, there are no people in this picture and the landscapes contain Archaic attributes in the heavy forms of stunted trees that squat along the base-line in Plate 8.2. The stage and backdrop effect, described in Chapter 7, divides the hill from the oval lake and trees and the multiple horizons have been overpainted black to look like cuts or channels that seem to enter a hole in the left-hand side of the work. I was reminded of the hole in the leaking chimney (Plate 7.4) and wondered if a black substance was draining away. On the horizon John had painted a row of fence posts, and it seemed that this painting might reflect a new sense of being 'within the pale'.

John had worked up this landscape with opaque paint, but the next work was painted more directly in transparent washes, more like a sketch of three leafless trees, showing an edge of green round the centre tree like the first haze of foliage in spring. Multiple horizons consistently lead the eye back to the distance, and the painting gives an impression of recessive space that is associated with the Traditional Massive style. John's imagination seems to be leading him towards recollections of the outer world. This painting was followed by an interesting landscape that seems to reflect his need for spatial relations in the subject as well as the style (Plate 8.3). John asked me how one might paint a causeway, so that the end of the road seemed to meet the distant shore. His intuitive sense of space had already provided the appropriate colour/tone needed for representing distance, but the narrow causeway between foreground and background seemed to epitomize the psychological difficulty of making the conscious transition. There was also a technical difficulty in making a consistent grading of the colour and tone in the narrow width of the receding road; this demanded that he use a close hand and eye coordination that he had not consciously contrived before. He was able to use my suggestion that the far end of the causeway road was given the same colour/tone as the distant shore; his conscious efforts to achieve this detail show as an awkward amateurishness that did not appear in any of his other work.

After this John's art seems to have established itself in the Traditional Massive mode for he effortlessly created a beautiful scene in pearly colours (Plate 8.4). This open landscape shows a river flowing past a heather-covered hillside. The paint has even applied directly, with little over-working, and the whole effect is simple and clear, in spite of the raindrops that had damaged it afterwards. The composition is subtle: the circle obscure, dominated by the horizontal demands of the subject matter. As usual, John did not comment on this work, but he showed his appreci-ation of my visit in a new concern for my comfort in the stormy weather – was my chair wet and would I like a cup of tea, if he could arrange for one to be brought? He certainly looked relaxed, and lay rather quietly, looking at his work. The painting of Plate 8.5 is incomplete. The landscape seems to incorporate some actual recollections in the particular shape of the distant mountain and the quality of the rock strata that he was working up in the foreground. He might have been painting when he was told that his doctors had decided he was well enough to travel home to Ireland. John's excitement was expressed in a quick sketch (Plate 8.6) in which the style reverted to the Massive Transition. The landscape shows a wide range of hills under a hazy sky. The clouds are lifted from the horizon and the sun shines darkly through them. There is a lake in the middle distance and the images in the foreground are separated from the general light and space by some emphatic details. A wavering line divides the 'stage' from the back-drop, although there is not a clear cut-off line between them. In the fore-ground a house goes up in flames, and a little fat man runs naked towards us past a green tree that rises up like a balloon from below the edge of the paper. On the right stand two strange creatures, perhaps they are a horse and a fowl. On this occasion I felt that I could ask John about the content of his painting. He readily replied, but was brief. 'The house is on fire but the man is out.' After a bit I asked about the animals and John replied, 'They're singed a bit, the man and the animals, but they're all right. I've painted a lot of water so they can jump in the lake!' Then he said that he would not be taking his paintings or the paints home with him and also handed back the unused sheets of paper. When I advised him to keep his work he said that there would be no place to put them, and I was welcome to any that I liked. John had signed some of his later works and seemed to expect that I would take one of these, but I was extremely pleased to have them all and found an X-ray box in which they could be safely stored.

The first time that John spontaneously achieved the Traditional Massive style in the picture of the smugglers (Plate 7.6), he was unable to sustain it. He was so angry that he felt that he could never paint again. At the time I wondered if his anger was directed at the doctor who, John thought, looked like the guarda, and if this anger concealed depression or a homosexual or sado-masochistic fantasy. Even if I had felt sure that this was what the painting showed, I could not hope to do more than heighten John's resistance if I tried to interpret this to him. I am glad that such an intervention was not possible because it would have diverted attention from the picture as a whole, the colours, tones and placement of the figures in space and the precipitous drop in the foreground that spoke non-verbally of his fears in the context of sadness and depression. Moreover, the subject matter seemed to extend the ideas that had began to surface in the previous picture of the men in the bog (Plate 7.5), in which John had found great difficulty in separating the hands of the sinking man from that of his companion. The idea that father and son are both engaged in a dangerous and illegal game seems to show another aspect of his preoccupation with death. The central smuggler has a skull-like head and the smuggled object looks like a coffin. The right hand figure, who looks like John himself, seems to recall an actual experience of lifting a heavy coffin.

The Traditional Massive style is created through perceptions or recollections of actual events that can be seen when the mind's eye is comparatively free of the childish fantasies of magic and anthropomorphism. When John painted men rather than dwarfs, giants or a cracked chimney, he showed his ability to mourn for past relationships with people and to have pity for himself. Although at first he regressed to the Massive Transitional style, when he started to paint again, he was able to recover the intuitive/perceptive attitude in other landscape paintings.

John's verbal uncommunicativeness was balanced by the rich and dynamic communications of his pictorial style. In spite of the ambiguousness of the subject matter in his pictures, I could follow his integrative efforts, and this gave a sense of rapport to my visits with him. For the final example of the Traditional Massive style I shall turn to the work of a boy who used stories and poems as much as paint and clay. I shall concentrate on the verbal aspect of his art as it deals with his particular need to perceive the external world and, in particular, his own outer self and its relation to reality.

Freddie was an exciting patient to work with because his creative drive impelled him to test out his magical expectations of invincibility through is art work and his stories and poems will show the tremendous efforts he made to integrate the inner and outer reality of his life.

Freddie was 11 years old, a small, physically immature child with bright, staring eyes and jerky, hyperactive movements. Sometimes he jumped about and flapped his hands. He had come into care with his brother when he was 6 years old, having been subjected to repeated violence and cruelty. He was invited to work in my studio once a week because he often lost his head and his violence, stealing and smoking were causing concern. To some of the staff he seemed strange and frightening. He was considered educationally subnormal and unlikely to join his brother in an ordinary secondary school as he wished. He had great difficulty in getting to sleep at night and often had nightmares. During the day he sometimes fell into 'staring fits' from which he woke, afraid that he was 'not all there'. The possibility of epilepsy was not considered.

Freddie's first weeks in therapy seemed ecstatic. He gesticulated strangely over the trays of paint and exclaimed passionately about the beauty of the colours – he felt he could do anything with them. He painted decisively, first choosing the colours and rarely mixing them. The style of his work was not inappropriate for his age: it varied from the Archaic Massive to the Massive Transition, and he adopted a few conventional representations, such as two distant hills with the sun shining between them. From the first he told stories about things he had painted or modelled: these ideas were often based on things he had learned at school, freely adapted to his own needs.

Freddie's modelling was exceptionally plastic; he had no difficulty in creating three-dimensional mass. His clay work seemed to anticipate the naturalism of the Traditional Massive style. His commitment to art was intense; he came for his session early, and remained hidden in the garden until the proper time and left reluctantly at the end. My examples of his work are drawn from the stories he dictated: some of these are in the form of poems. He tended to use recurring themes; one important series was about a dangerous, but friendly animal, the rhino. Perhaps the most important stories were about boats, which I will describe now. He had painted a river flowing between two mountains. The style was Massive Transitional and the colours black, royal blue for the water, white and harsh green. As always, he dictated the story, which he called *The Indian and his boat*:

> Once upon a time there was a little Indian that always wanted to have a boat. So he hadn't got the money to buy one so one day he found some pieces of old wood and he made a boat and he tried to see if it worked but he forgot the paddles and he went in the sea and suddenly his memory came back to him, and he thought he was going to make another boat but decided not to. 'When this one breaks I will make a stronger one and go out and fish in the sea.'

Freddie seemed to be telling himself about his absences of mind and his plans for dealing with this at a later time, and also, perhaps that he could not 'paddle his own canoe'. The story seems to break off when the little Indian's memory came back to him. I did not know if he escaped from the river or merely stayed where he was and thought about it. This break in the sequence of events seemed like the break-off angle of the Massive Transitional style of stage and backdrop in his painting. The boat is actually painted in the foreground, on the shore. A few weeks later Freddie came with an exciting story he had heard at school about a man who caught a 'colio-fish' (coelacanth). It seemed so marvellous to Freddie that something unknown could be brought up from under the sea that he rushed about the studio, jumping and madly gesticulating as he prepared the paper and paint, choosing black, white, brown and royal blue. He first painted a background of black and white mountains with a large circle of royal blue water in the middle distance. On this lake he carefully drew a small rowing boat in brown paint, shown in profile. Below it he made a similar shape in reverse, which he filled with crossed lines, representing a net. This painting was called *The fisherman*, although the boat was empty. Freddie dictated a poem in a sing-song voice:

> One day there was a big big sky,
> Beneath it was a whole lot of mountains,
> And there was a big blue sun
> and a big red sea.
>
> There was a little ship
> sailing by the sea,
> it had red sails,
> and the colour of the boat itself
> was yellow.
>
> The man who was in the boat
> Was fishing for a fish.
> But, he didn't catch any fish.
>
> He waited and waited
> For the fish to come but –
> They would not come.
>
> Soon the man's birthday came
> and he went out in his boat once more.
> He caught lots and lots of fish for his family
> He had so many fish he had to sell some,
> And then he became a millionaire.

Freddie seems to have discovered the coelacanth as a symbolic image of creative initiative – a wonderful discovery from the depths of the unconscious reverie. In this mood his world is full of colour and the boat has a sail. However, the story tells him that this fantasy runs far ahead of his own ability: the fisherman must wait and wait before he can catch fish. Freddie needs a birthday – to be born as an integrated whole. As soon as he had completed the poem he began to plan a puppet, collecting some pieces of dowelling and paint rags that were lying about. This project occupied him for several sessions. When he found that wood was too difficult to carve he made the feet and hands of clay. He sawed the dowelling, made joints of string and sewed clothes and modelled a head. He was quite sure that the puppet would seem like a real person, and when he found that he could not work the strings to make it move in a life-like way he simply cut them off and played happily with it as it lay flat on the table. At first the puppet was called Wurzel Gummidge, after a comic character in a television programme, but then he renamed it as 'a tall man'. Freddy dictated a story about him to me, called *The statue*:

> A good man lived for many years and then he died. And the people thought that he was valuable to them now so they worshipped him as a god. And there was an even bigger statue – and he was the king of China! The people asked Freddie to make a grand statue of the good old man and so Freddie took some red clay and shaped it and carved it and made a face with ears, and he took white clay for the hair and when it was finished – it was done.

In this story Freddie seemed to discover that his need for a 'good old man' led to idealization, a statue like a god that he could make as he made the puppet. His style of telling the story was rather like his use of the puppet when he cut off the animating strings. When the image had been made, it was finished – 'it was done'.

When the puppet was finished Freddie returned to the story of the fisherman and made another painting, almost identical to the first; however, he added a pale blue sky and the mountains were white and rounded and without the black streaks that had been given to them in the original picture. A dead tree was painted on the left bank. The lake filled the lower part of the painting, down to the lower edge, and the boat was very small, painted in dark brown. It lay in the path of the sun's rays and the shape of the boat is inverted below it. This picture gave rise to another story called *The shadow*:

> One day there was a boat. It was a very small fishing boat and it never seemed to see its shadow, so, on one very dull day the boat went out to the pond and there was no shadow! 'Why isn't there a shadow?' said the boat. And the wind blew and blew and the boat went home. The man who owned the boat was a young fisherman; he usually talked to the boat because there was nothing else to do. One sunny morning the boat went out. The boat had never had a fish in it before and it had never saw its shadow before, and the boat was so glad to see its shadow. He was so glad that he turned into a giant fisherman-boat and the fisherman was so glad that he turned into a millionaire. And from that day they would only go out on a summer day. That's all.

Freddie ended his story with his usual burst of elation, but then he became absorbed in reverie. Eventually he asked me if I would write down some-thing else: 'The shadow was itself it had never seen before and that's what its dream was. . . . The grey was coming at them so they had to get into the pond.'

I could not be sure what Freddie meant, but it seemed as if the story might be connected with the memory of escaping 'into the grey' as an image of the abstractions that sometimes overtook him. As usual, I longed to understand more but could not feel that questions were appropriate at that time. He was working freely, and that was the most important thing.

Freddie was entering his twelfth year, and it seemed a race against time if he was not to become labelled as a delinquent. There had been many improvements, for he was not stealing, and vicious fighting was rare; his teachers found that his concentration had improved, and it seemed that he would be able to join his older brother at secondary school. However, Freddie's carers felt the urgency of his social problems and intensified their efforts to control him, feeling that practical necessities should take precedence over attention to the times of profound abstraction and depersonalization that continued to undermine their efforts.

In some poems Freddie tried to understand the inflated moods that led to many dangerous and violent acts. Here is such a poem that developed from a painting he had made of a brightly coloured balloon, to which he had added thick brown lines as guy-ropes. He chanted:

One day there was a big balloon.
The big balloon was very, very big.
And it had an owner.
And the owner said,
I will take you up in the sky today,
To see what you are like.
It's only a test
So you needn't worry
And you can wave,
About in the sky.
It's your only chance now,
Because we are ready for the circus tomorrow.

This poem pleased me as it carries a consistent sense of time, the flight today included a sense of its effect upon tomorrow. It seems to show a deep awareness of his problem and his precarious position in the children's home where, if he did not meet their requirements, the balloon would, indeed go up! The poem made me hopeful that inner and outer reality might become integrated, providing there was enough support for him during the next few years. The big balloon appeared to be a circle of self and perhaps the guy-ropes – lines of force – were emanating from the circle rather than imposed upon it. It is not only a beautiful balloon but lively, able to take some initiative and wave about in the sky if the owner (Freddie's self, or myself perhaps?) gives permission. It is possible that the owner, and the guy-ropes were becoming internalized, but these developments were tragically interrupted by the unexpected death of his father.

At first it seemed that he could mourn for the daddy who had given him a mouth-organ when he was six, but there were very few memories of this kind to counter his terrible fantasies. The ghostly world closed in on him and he struggled to protect himself from poisonous snakes and skeletons. He visited his father's grave to pray but could only feel that he had to dig him up. He modelled a little coffin in clay, working with care and precision. It was embellished with tiny handles and Freddie told me that the lid had a brass plate on it with his name and his brother's name on it. He hoped that people would not try to open the lid: it couldn't be opened for he had sealed it up. Eventually he was unable to contain his horrors in our work together and confided them to his brother, who forbad him to think such dreadful things or to continue to work with me. This seemed the last straw: Freddie added burglary to his crimes and had to leave the children's home.

Miss Rink, John and Freddie have helped me to understand the therapeutic importance of space/time representation in the Traditional Massive style. Miss Rink showed me its limitations. The difference between the Archaic and Traditional styles might be thought about in terms of Freud's pleasure principle and reality principle, except for the fact that both views have equal reality and pleasure attached to them. Both are necessary to defend the self from monopoly by one aspect or the other when they are exercised by the patient in a therapeutic setting. Traditional Massive art reflects the outer world and satisfies a need for emotional detachment through a displacement of feelings upon impersonal objects – mountains and rivers, chimneys and boats; finally it concerns itself with the abstract qualities of distance, its space and light. As an habitual attitude of relation to others it can lead to a loss of self-value and even individual choice, as Edward's depression showed me; this seemed to me a pathological regression, as in John's larky indifference to his dangerous illness and even the more extreme loss of Freddie in dissociated states.

Therapy demands movement, and art materials provide the means of locomotion. Miss Rink needed her therapeutic regression with the big Archaic sun and John needed to go back to the Archaic images that he might have conceived when he was only a few years old. Freddie had to choose colours and use them rather than wave his hands in ecstasy above the whole glittering trayful. The first colours he used were deathly cold. His poems and stories told of his efforts to reach the images of space and time he needed to contain the magical and anthropomorphic view of life that had led to conflict with his carers.

In summary, the Traditional Massive style draws attention to the outer world, and the overriding effect that light and space impose upon colours, tones and forms. Its psychological message is clear: we are related to others when we live with apperceptions of space and time.

Figure 9.1 *Higson's roundabout* Traditional Transition

Chapter 9

The Traditional Transition
Surface reality and idealism

We continue to follow the styles that make up the Traditional half of the circle of styles. These present a more or less familiar view of life even though the subject matter may be extraordinary. The transition links the Traditional Massive appearances of naturalistic representation with the formal constructs of conceptual art. I will describe something of the successes and failures of the integrative impulse that underlies its typical appearance.

THE APPEARANCE

This art is generally considered naturalistic. However, it is not an indiscriminate reflection of our perceptions of the outer world but emphasizes the separateness of each part. Nothing is allowed to be obscured or overshadowed as it would be in reality. This distinctness gives an exaggerated effect, as if each part had been studied under a magnifying glass. The boundaries of shapes are clearly defined by their contrasting colour or tone, such as the separate features of a face (Figure 9.2).

POSTURE AND GESTURE

The artist perfects his representations by focusing upon each part separately. He does not use the boundary of his canvas like a window giving a single, unified view but completes one section at a time. His posture is freed from a fixed relation to the work, which is no longer tied to his body's limitations. The work is less an emanation of the artist than his object and he works at it piecemeal. In this way huge paintings can be made in sections and the disjointed effect disguised by working from a small sketch that can be mechanically enlarged.

REVERIE AND FANTASY

The style of any spontaneous work reflects the unconscious reverie that shapes its form. Traditional art that combines formal with perceptual elements images an impulse towards integration of thought and external reality, an impulse to order nature and give it meaning. Perfect examples are sought and perhaps the most fully documented development of idealism was written at the time of the Italian Renaissance. Neo-platonic idealism had been rationalized into theories of aesthetics, and the ideal of essence was interpreted as knowledge. Artists sought complete knowledge of their subjects by turning to history and geography, mathematics, geology, astronomy, and, particularly, geometry. The art of measurement seemed to many artists to hold the key to art's perfection. Perfect proportion was sought in the composition of paintings, sculptures and architecture; artists concerned themselves with the complexities of geometric perspective. The Gothic ideal of art as the servant of God was replaced by the attempt to make art the servant of man's intellect. However, even the greatest artists were not able to contain all the available knowledge in their art. The unconscious demand for integration of inner with outer reality persisted. For example, although the laws of perspective might be used in place of visual or emotional arbiters of distance, a picture did not necessarily give an impression of space. Theory could make nonsense of art, and vice versa, as we see in a detail from *Hunt in the forest* painted by Paolo Uccello (Figure 9.3). As an example of his genius it is a slight, superficial work, and it is difficult to imagine that the great artist of the trilogy, *The rout of San Romano*, did not intend the panel (which seems to have been part of a clothes chest) to be a joke against the strictures of the new scientific act of perspective. As we study the painting it is clear that the vanishing points do not enable things to vanish into the distance. However far away in the forest the hunters are supposed to be, the bright red of their tunics leaps forward to the eye. Each man and beast has been spotlighted by colour or tone contrast against his background and there is no single source of light. Moreover, if we try to relate the parts of the scene together in terms of geometric perspective we find that the details have been conceived separately, without any regard for the space that they would be supposed to occupy. The detail of the horse in Figure 9.3 is taken from the extreme right side of the panel. It is shown as foreshortened, but since its feet are in parallel with the tree it must be about to collide with it; moreover with all its feet in this position the great beast could not balance, but would fall over. Perhaps *Hunt in the forest* shows the conflict between Uccello's love of voluminous masses, such as the horse, and his interest in the new, *dolce* perspective.

Many artists of the Renaissance were aware of the limitations that intellectual disciplines such as perspective had set upon their creative imagination. Leonardo da Vinci wrote: 'It should not be too difficult sometimes to stop and look into stains on walls, ashes in the fire, or clouds, or mud or like places in which you may find really marvellous ideas' (Clarke 1963: 82).

Figure 9.2 *Head of a girl* Traditional Transition

Figure 9.3 A detail of *Hunt in the forest*, by Paolo Uccello, Traditional Transition

Reproduced by permission of the Ashmolean Museum, Oxford

Botticelli's method of achieving free fantasy was also by looking outward, following the same principle of accidental effects rather more vigorously: 'by merely throwing a sponge full of paint at a wall it leaves a blot where one sees a fine landscape' (Gombrich 1990: 160).

From the art style we can surmise the unconscious image as a circle in a square that contains an unbroken surface that has a levelling effect upon all its parts. The fantasies shown by the subject matter are also without depth for feelings in the whole area of sensuous and emotional life are constrained to express the rational sentiments that are commonly held. It seems as if the circle asserts itself against such dissolution by the hard edge of idealism that is the hallmark of classical art. If it leads too far from the world of everyday appearances the art splits off into mannerism or conventional artifice.

THE SYMBOLISM

If there is continuing conflict between perceived reality and idealism the Traditional Transition undergoes a subtle change in appearance. The

polished technique and definition comes to conceal illogical and contra-
dictory features. On the one hand the artist has an unconscious assumption
of space as two-dimensional, where everything in outer reality is equally
perfect and complete. This conflicts with a sophisticated grasp of three-
dimensional reality that can be rationally explained by geometric perspective. As a result an image may be remembered, or even perceived as
composite. Figure 9.1 is an example of this confusion of the two Traditional
styles in an attempt to show that the animals are all round *Higson's roundabout.* As a result the running board on the carousel is presented as an
'impossible image' (Gregory 1966: 226).

THERAPY

The positive use of this transition can be found in its power to draw out the
artist's intellectual discrimination, his knowledge and skill in recognizing
the external world. This allows him to copy and repeat surface appearances
at times when he needs release from intolerable ambiguities or inconsist-
encies. The style can be used like a cleansing wind over a clouded landscape. Edward, described in Chapter 8, found a solution to his depressed
state in this way. The artist reaches beyond the sticks and stones of his
actual experience to invent instruments or techniques that will reach further
to a sense of some absolute quality of life. In Edward's case there was
movement from the Traditional Massive style towards the Traditional
Linear; however, when a patient's habitual attitude has been sustained by
his striving for perfection, there is less likelihood that he will use art as a
therapy. It is very hard for those who have lived in aspiration for a long
time to recognize meaning in spontaneous activity, especially when they
have suffered a breakdown of these ideals. These patients are serious,
thorough and sometimes obsessive people who do not play. If they have
some technical skill in recreating art the creative impulse may obtrude
Archaic elements into their work that are unnerving; in consequence their
concern with skill is redoubled and the content narrowed down to the
barest representational stereotypes: almost invariably the patient gives up
any attempt to create art.

DEPRESSION IN THE TRADITIONAL TRANSITION

Now I need to describe the particular approach to therapy concerning the
depression experienced by patients who use this style. First of all I need to
consider the patient's situation very carefully, as failure to use art creatively
might become the last straw that breaks down his defences. I need to pay
attention to the pace of the work and measure this by the intervals between
sessions in relation to the patient's situation, the support and attention he is
getting from his home or hospital and the possibility of a physical illness

that might lower his defence or signal his need for extra care. Elsewhere I have described the quiet resolve with which this type of depression may cause him to end his life (Simon 1972). Consequently I have few examples of works that might give warning of suicide. Hospitalized patients who are directed to an art therapy group may take a very long time to free themselves from a need for absolute standards. One might see this in terms of an over-strict superego that has imposed a double standard of self-determination under the rule of absolute compliance to the ego ideal. When a patient shows extreme rigidity and an open hostility to creative work, I cannot believe that he should be persuaded to try. However, I have seen thera-

Figure 9.4 *The piper* Traditional Transition

peutic change in the art style of a 70-year-old patient who recovered from depression during the time when her style spontaneously changed, freed of the discipline of a line and wash technique. At one stage of her recovery, the spaces between objects were left unpainted and even colour was omitted: hard outlines merged with massive, crudely painted forms. *The piper* (Figure 9.4) is an example of her new-found ability to allow some incompleteness and vulnerability to depression to be expressed in the Traditional Massive style. This lady had previously described her mental state to me as 'a shoddy framework of despair'.

There are a few occasions when it is right for the therapist to risk a suggestion. A patient had painted a very rigid picture of a garden in winter and I noticed that in it a small pond reflected the trailing branches of a willow. The thin branches and soft colour contrasted with the quality of the rest of the painting and I felt that they showed the tentative emergence of the Traditional Massive style. I decided to suggest that she painted the view that might be hidden by the picture frame. She took up this idea and painted the view that might be seen beyond the fence as a wide vista of warm sunny hills. In the distance a church and churchyard could be seen distinctly as a part of the scene. It seemed that this painting was concerned with the place of bereavement in her life.

Two further examples are given to show the precariousness of the will to live that is expressed in this style when the habitual attitude of self-control breaks down.

A middle-aged woman was admitted to hospital after attempting suicide following the unexpected death of her husband and business partner. When she had seemed to recover she was advised to follow a programme of rehabilitation which included sessions in the hospital art therapy group. She was a composed, well-groomed lady but seemed coldly indifferent to the opportunity to draw or paint. Eventually she moved to a worktable and made a small watercolour of a backless wooden bench, using brown and green lines. The small brush-drawing was isolated in the centre of a large piece of paper. This work was soon completed and she returned to a chair at the side of the room. During the following weekend she was allowed home for a second visit and there killed herself, using equipment that she had purchased the week before.

The second patient, Jean, was younger: a quiet, unassuming housewife who appeared sad and apathetic rather than negative. She was offered a place in a weekly outpatient group and at first I found her indefinably difficult to contact. She did not complain of depression, but of asthma. She painted easily, first making a conventional flower-piece that she might have reproduced many times before, assembled in parts like vignettes from a gardening catalogue. The Traditional transitional style gave the work no sense of space or colour harmony. Its surface appearance of neat control seemed in contrast to Jean's quiet evasiveness. The following week she was

Figure 9.5 *Church gardens* Massive Transition

more responsive and told me that she had found a new sense of peace while sitting by herself in the gardens of a church, talking to a cat. I suggested that she might like to make use of this good experience as the starting point for a painting. Perhaps I was too eager to get in touch with her feelings and distract her from her stereotyped approach to art. Jean took the idea literally and painted a view of the garden and the church in the distance (Figure 9.5). At first this was a Traditional Massive painting but as the work progressed the sense of distance was upset and the style changed to the more Archaic Transition. The darkened overpainting of the church projected it forward and with the empty foreground gave an impression of a stage and backdrop. In this short time Jean told me that she was enjoying painting and it seemed to help her breathing. She described her decision to overpaint the church with a stronger brown and the feeling of strength that the buttresses gave to the building. She drew my attention to the noticeboard, saying that it looked remarkably real, and she decided to add coloured glass to the windows. I was very pleased to see how much Jean had been able to develop her imagination in this work. I wondered to myself whether this experience could help her by its suggestion of a religious solution to her suffering.

Figure 9.6 *Swan* Traditional Transition

During her work on this painting Jean was often deeply absorbed. She continued this picture for several sessions and on one occasion whispered to me her growing concern about the effect of her health on her life as a mother of several young children. Then her sessions were interrupted while she had to be home with the children for several weeks. When she did return I was away for a week and the group was led by a nurse. The nurse noticed that Jean seemed exhausted and depressed; however, she started a small painting of a swan (Figure 9.6) but did not complete the foreground. Before the end of the week she had taken an overdose of drugs and was dead.

For a patient such as Jean, particular attention is needed to consider the defensive aspect of an habitual attitude and the extent to which the therapeutic setting can provide an equivalent sense of security. With hindsight it was obvious that the conditions of outpatient group work were totally inadequate for Jean. A patient's apathy or coldness of manner may be his last means of defence against the demands of the inner world. The therapist must wait as long as necessary before the habitual attitude can be relaxed and creative work begin. During the waiting time such a patient may find the ordinary circumstances of everyday life intolerable and need to be totally cared for until a therapeutic alliance can be properly established. Once spontaneous art work is underway the therapist can follow the pattern of self-healing, whether it is moving towards an intuitive integration or whether a more down-to-earth thinking attitude releases the patient from unthinking idealism and compliance.

Finally, I will compare the content, style and symbolic imagery in Jean's painting of the church garden (Figure 9.5). The content is limited by the little that Jean told me about it. However, the style and symbolism contribute to our understanding of this work. It was a surprise to me and a pleasure to see because it was so much more expressive than the rigid little flower-pieces that she had seemed to make only to comply with her family's need to prove that she was not ill. I was impressed by the extent of the fantasy in the church garden picture, indicated by the time she spent on the painting and the alterations she made to it. Her freedom to change and overpaint her picture suggested that she had freed herself from the self-limiting perfection of the earlier art work that had prevented her from introducing anything original. As her painting progressed, the Traditional Massive style was partly lost by the overpainting of the church with heavy, warm colours and tones. These disturbed the spatial illusion so that the style regressed to the Massive Transition. By this I guessed that Jean had extended positive feelings during her painting and located them in the image of the church. In particular, the addition of a brightly-lit window in the tower gave the effect of a single figure in a circle of crimson glass, in strong contrast to the empty flowerbed in the cool-coloured gardens.

Jean left this painting in her folder when it was finished. I wondered if this meant that she did not feel that it would be so acceptable at home as the earlier work. In fact the painting was a therapeutic regression. Content, style and symbolic imagery all show her search for emotional reality. The content can be compared to Miss Rink's *Seascape* (Plate 1.3) which also seems to balance good and bad images; but Miss Rink had finally flung a huge Archaic sun into her orderly, rational painting and upset the balance with the deeper, irrational truth that 'Naught loves another as itself, or venerates another so' (Blake 1939: 33).

In terms of the basic symbolism of the Circle in Square, I was a little bothered by the sides of Jean's painting, for the leafless trees show empty spaces between them, painted like patches of sky. This gives an effect of placing the garden in limbo. These empty gaps in the square might be compared with Pippi's fragmented circles in *'The Big I'* (Figure 3.6), indicating a need for a boundary and the inadequacy of Jean's own efforts to contain herself without help.

Jean's work might be crudely interpreted as presenting the rival claims of the inner and outer world. The content puts this as a question: how much could she stay out in the cold and how much in the warmth of a shared community, indicated by the lighted windows of the church? The style augments this question: how much does she need contact with the latency view of the Massive Transition and how much with the Traditional Massive intuitive perception of a life that seemed dead wood and broken branches? Jean spoke of painting with pleasure, and said that it helped her breathing. Perhaps the painting had provided a breathing space in which these questions could have been worked out if there had been sufficient time.

VISUAL ILLUSIONS

Working with patients who use a Traditional Transition, I have found that some of them have extraordinary experiences that may cut across the apathy and negative compliance that makes these patients difficult to help. Such experiences might be loosely collected under the idea of positive and negative illusions, or hallucinations. Some patients do describe them as hallucinations; however, they do not seem to have the unquestionable authenticity of an hallucination but are open to consideration in a therapeutic setting. Although I cannot say that such experiences are only met by the attitude that is expressed in the Traditional Transitional style, I only hear of them when they can be linked to thinking and talked about. For this very reason they do not seem true hallucinations. They occur at times of abstraction or dissociation, when a sudden recall to outer reality seems to be confused with fantasy. A patient may impose abstract shapes or colours upon a conventional representation, indicating the disjunction between perceptions and thoughts. For example, one member of an art therapy day hospital group always painted Traditional Linear representations of still life or abstract patterns, set within the frame of a triangle. Outside this area she placed scattered letters and geometric shapes. When another patient asked her what this writing meant she muttered that it did not mean anything – she didn't know what it meant. In time her style changed to the Traditional Transition, and then, when looking back over her earlier work she was able to tell me that the meaningless ciphers represented things that her psychiatrist had told her. At that time she felt that she could not understand what he was saying or even see him properly when he stood before her with his hand in his pocket. She could only look through the triangle made by the gap between his body and his bent elbow. It seemed that she had almost created a negative hallucination, for the outline of the inner arm and the doctor's body had been painted as a meaningless frame for her pictures. The only things visible at that moment were seen through the crook of his arm; apparently she had used her eyes as well as her ears to blot him out.

Another patient struggled to maintain a balance between a perceptual memory and her ideas after painting a similar experience of illusion. This young woman, Myra, was not altogether considered to be schizophrenic, but she had a history of borderline hysterical illnesses. On one occasion she came to the hospital outpatient art group in panic, insisting that the street outside was full of male and female soldiers and armoured cars. I could not immediately give her the time she needed, for the group was demanding attention, so I asked her to paint her experience to help me to understand what she had actually seen. Myra chose white paper and first drew the picture carefully in pencil, then she added heraldic colours of khaki and grey. Although she normally painted in the Traditional Massive style, this work was Traditional Transition (Figure 9.7). The figures and cars were separated by unpainted areas, and only the figure representing herself was given some spacial relation and distinguished by the blue colour of her dress. By the time that the work was completed Myra's mood had changed. She raised the question of the armoured cars herself. She explained that the cars she had painted were not the same as those she now remembered seeing in the street! With this beautiful insight we could follow the actual process of transformation from the disturbance of her thoughts to the rational and verbal discrimination made possible through her pictorial representation of the scene. Every part of Myra's picture represents the thought distortion upon her perception: the flat, two-dimensional effect of shops without depth, ground without space and figures encapsulated, each separated from the others by an area of white paper like a cloud. As we studied the painting I wondered about the implications of the tight little red handbags that all the figures carried.

Verbal interpretation of a living experience, however strange, is like a dissection. The dead thing that our words leave with us can easily make the experience seem more strange or mad than it actually is. Guided by her painting, Myra came to understand her experience by degrees. We both

Figure 9.7 *Armoured cars* Traditional Transition

needed time to look at the picture in silence as her mood slowly altered and her recollection of the sensuous reality of the experience changed to a rational attempt to understand what had happened to her. Fortunately it had been possible to arrange for a session later on the same day. In its own time the definitive nature of verbal thought played an important part in her understanding, but Myra also needed to pursue the creative aspect of the hallucination as a vision of her inner reality as well as a distorted view of a busy street. Dialogue was needed between the inner and outer worlds. It would have been simpler for her to have denied one of them. As a hysteric or schizophrenic she could have remained mad, insisting on the reality of the hallucination, or she might have denied any reality at all to her experience. Painting gave her the essential time she needed to stay with her immediate recollection until she was able to see, in the little figure in the blue dress, the unconscious preoccupation with her body self and its indifference to the outer world at such times. Perhaps the act of crossing the road had awakened her from her dreamy self-absorption and she was suddenly made aware of danger – a real danger from the traffic. The illusion, or hallucination that Myra experienced in the here-and-now of a busy road could be seen as a projection of her visual thought about her vulnerability to sensuous preoccupations and the dissociating effect of their repression.

SUMMARY

This particular area of transition connects the Massive and Linear aspects of Traditional art. The underlying attitude of intuitive perception is combined with conscious notions and thoughts. The unconscious reverie seems to hold the symbolic image of circle in square as divided into parts that are equally perfect and a complete interlocking surface. The fantasies that develop from this unconscious image form ideal standards of beauty and truth. If such assumptions about the nature of reality become fixed as an habitual attitude, the individual's inner world is deprived of creative initiative. Art and life have been stereotyped and become progressively devoid of meaning. Eventually the idealistic framework collapses, causing a type of depression associated with indifference, apathy and exhaustion. If art materials can be used as a means of therapeutic regression there is an opportunity for new integrations to be visualized and the danger of suicidal despair to be averted.

Figure 10.1 Egyptian Tomb Painting, *The garden pool,* Traditional Linear
Reproduced by permission of the Trustees of the British Museum, London

Chapter 10

The Traditional Linear style
Visual and verbal thinking

In this chapter I shall present a style that seems to bridge images and rational thoughts in ways that have particular advantages and limitations. In the previous chapter some of these effects were described as modified by the particular form of emotion that we call idealism; here the attitude seems detached. Thinking about something enables us to separate out its special properties in the same way that outlines can be used to distinguish an image from its background. This gives a piecemeal effect to an art work. I am clearest in my thoughts when I can find words to fit them, and when I need to communicate precisely I must use words, even when talking to myself. By comparison, visual thinking is like shorthand, an *aide-mémoire* that escapes the ponderous structure of grammar and syntax. The synchronicity of a visualization may appear as inspiration; for example, Kekule's famous Benzine ring (Koestler 1970: 117–18). In lesser ways it can be used to resolve mental conflict. An example from my own life may be useful here.

When I was considering the possibility of a personal analysis I could not at first weigh the hoped-for advantages against the effect of considering art from a different point of view (from its aesthetic value). At the time I hesitated to take a step that seemed drastically to affect myself as a professional artist. One night as I lay half asleep I suddenly saw in my mind's eye a distinct image of a huge bee, flying towards the round wall of an old-fashioned well. The bee was distinctly seen, its legs, wings and furry body flew close to my face; the well was some feet away, entangled in brambles, weeds and flowers. The images were so clear and attractive that I was fully awakened and it occurred to me that they represented a visual pun that I deciphered as 'well-be'. These syllables were the first part of the telephone code I had to use when my decision had been made; moreover, when reversed it suggested the idea that I might be well to take up the offer. I used this day-dream, in a relaxed state between sleeping and waking, as a directive, even though that might not have been the reason for its appearance.

Such experiences as this seem to be advocated by Jung and developed as a therapy based on a guided imagery that tends to attract a mood of free-flowing thought that is typified by the Traditional Linear style. However, verbal thinking is not solely imaged by this style but is available to all the Traditional styles. For example, the day-dream I have described was formed by a naturalistic image shown moving through space – typical qualities of the Traditional Massive style. Perhaps the quality of visual thought can be compared with the dominance of emotions and sensuous experiences in the Archaic modes by describing the latter as being capable of being thought about but not formed with thought. The relative detachment that pervades the Traditional styles allowed me to enjoy the dream without any anxiety about the proximity of the huge insect or the derelict appearance of the well. Years after, my state of amused realization allowed me to tune in to Chris's relief when he recognized the significance of his diagrammatic sketch of the *Lysistrata* stage set (Figure 2.4) and the containing strength of the *Bronchoscopy* painting (Plate 1.4) that faced the traumatic experience.

THE APPEARANCE

The naturalistic representation of images is subjected to formal definition of meaning. Shape dominates over form, colour is also used to indicate distinctions and objects presented in line, from the familiar point of view. The scale is small and the effect stylized, orderly and may contain carica-ture. If geometric perspective is used it presents an idea of recession but not the appearance of it and, in general, an art work can be paraphrased without losing anything of importance. This conceptualization of images allows them to be repeated and stereotyped; it may reduce the work to a mere pictograph, limited to a single meaning. Figure 10.1 is a charming example of the style. The pond is presented in plan so that we can see the fish inside and the surrounding trees are folded back so that they do not obscure the view.

POSTURE AND GESTURE

This style reflects the limitations that are adopted by all who learn to use the close coordination of hand and eye demanded in handwriting. The posture is cramped, for the shoulder and arm of the active hand are con-tinually tensed. Support is needed for the hand by shifting along the working surface and the artist cannot continue for long without strain. He may try to overcome these difficulties by technical means and inventions that will take the strain from the work. He plans and prepares for the final work.

REVERIE AND FANTASY

There is little chance of spontaneous art work under these conditions; fantasy seems almost totally adopted by conscious intention and manipulated to carry out an anticipated result. The unconscious component of creative initiative lies in abeyance during the work process, although it may be discerned after it has been finished, as it was when the conscious intention to illustrate the traumatic experience of a bronchoscopy revealed the underlying cause of the artist's revulsion (Plate 1.4). Some works in the Traditional Linear style are abstract and in these it seems there can be direct contact with the basic symbolism of the circle as an image of the self within the area of the containing square. These designs may also become objects for contemplation in thoughts directed and given shape in terms of a mandala. Without the basic structure of circle in square the imagery is consciously shaped by ideas that may only repeat the limitations of verbal thought. Any interpretation of images will limit their associations still further and curtail the potential for change and growth.

In this style the unconscious reverie may be deduced from the linear segmentation of its images, which acts like the leading of coloured glass in a church window or like the brass divisions that separate the enamels in *cloisonné* work. Some artists are at pains to disguise the conceptual structure of their work, blurring the outlines later to imitate natural appearances to some extent, rather as a crackle glaze was developed to mimic the effect of a fault in firing. Blake seems to have had a particular hatred of such sophistications and assumed that all naturalistic art was a grave form of deception:

This Lifes five Windows of the Soul
Distorts the Heavens from Pole to Pole
And leads you to Believe a Lie
When you see with, not thro' the Eye. (Blake 1939: 350)

Traditional Linear fantasy projects the whole of reality upon the material world and deems it comprehensible down to its smallest details. Nothing seems beyond the reach of thought, and science has developed this vision through our ability to repress emotion during this state of mind.

THE SYMBOLISM OF THE TRADITIONAL ASPECT OF LINE

Line in this style is used to define the boundaries of shapes and contain them within clearly limited areas. We can speak of outlining our ideas and of the need to draw the line when our feelings threaten to get out of control. Such metaphors are visual images in Traditional Linear art, enabling the artist to contain his preconscious fantasy in an orderly, logical relation between discrete shapes that can be moved about and redrawn at will. The artist can plan, design and control all the parts of his work in this way. Line depersonalizes the reflective image, which is no longer shaped by inner necessity but bounded by a rational objective. Blake understood the symbolism of line:

> The more distinct, sharp and wiry the bounding line, the more perfect the work of art; and the less keen and sharp the greater is the evidence of imitation, plagiarism and bungling ... Leave out this line, and you leave out life itself: all is chaos again.
>
> (Blake, quoted in Raine 1970: 109–10)

This bounding line was Blake's means of creating order from chaos, but presumably he did not see it as only a bond or a boundary, but as a living, 'bounding' line.

The German expressionist, Georg Grosz, was most emphatic about the fear that can cause an artist to depend upon the linear boundary for his art:

> There must have been a reason for the invention of line. Yes, it is a guide for those who would venture into the formlessness that surrounds us on every side; a guide that leads us to the recognition of form and dimension and inner meaning. It is like the thread that Ariadne gave Theseus before he ventured into the mysterious recesses of the Labyrinth. Line guides us when we would enter the Labyrinth of countless millions of natural objects that surround us. Without line we should soon be lost: never would we be able to find our way out again.   (Grosz 1963)

Marion Milner, under the pseudonym of Joanna Field, (1950: 16) sums up these ideas as 'a fear of what might happen if one let go of one's mental hold upon outline which kept everything separate and in its place'.

THE STYLE AS THERAPY

I associate the Traditional Linear style with the omnipotence of pure thought, and its linear emphasis with fear of annihilation by the unconscious realities of sensuous and emotional life. Creative art may be used by a patient to extend his control over those fears or to transcribe emerging visions, illusions, hallucinations or hypnogogic impressions into rational meanings. My experience of the image of a bee and a well, described earlier, is a case in point. It might be said that conceptualization reduces the implications of the infinite meaning that is held within the basic symbol of the circle in the square, limiting it to a sign or cipher, a single idea. Such diminution of the creative potential of symbolic images might be essential for a patient emerging from the sterility of outward ideals, or for another who was suffering from the chaos of 'countless millions of natural objects'. However, a great artist such as Blake delineates in order to transcend materialism, by stripping appearances of light and shade, space and time, he presents the eternal in a temporal form.

The precariousness of abstract thought is fully appreciated by the artist Fernand Leger.

Abstract art is dominated by the same desire for complete and absolute freedom and perfection which inspires saints, heroes and madmen. It is a peak on which only a few creative artists and their admirers can maintain themselves. In fact the very danger of this peak is the rarified air by which it is surrounded.

Describing the appearance of abstract art, Leger lists 'respect for the vertical plane – thin, rigid, limiting ... true purism, incorruptible ... emerging coldly from chaos' (Leger 1963).

Patients who are obsessively practised in thinking may have tremendous difficulties in using an art form in which shapes are not absolutely determined. One individual became unbearably anxious when he could not mix 'the colour of grass'. It did not help to show him that grass has many colours and tones. However, the limiting, metaphorical effect of Traditional Linear art can have therapeutic effectiveness in cases where an habitual attitude is less inflexible. Alec was a sensitive and intelligent young professional who had to undergo a bronchoscopy. This simple, if unpleasant, diagnostic procedure had a most disturbing consequence: Alec could not overcome the feelings of revulsion that it had aroused in him. As I was working in the same hospital he asked to see me and to use some art materials as a way of mastering his feelings. I was able to provide the materials, time and setting in which he could paint. He set to work, carefully mixing a light blue wash of colour that filled the main area of the paper, which he framed with a wide grey boundary line. Then he drew a pair of spectacles and copied them onto the background colour. These he connected to a thin red tube that extended diagonally across the paper and appeared to enter a brown, irregular shape that he intended to represent his lung (Plate 1.4). At the top of this shape he carefully painted a small circular area, half-filled with red, which seemed to show the diseased spot on his lung, but its position transformed the brown shape to that of a female head and torso. This limbless, helpless body is penetrated by the bronchoscope in the region of the mouth. Alec could see that his phobic reaction was not merely a cowardly response to pain and discomfort, but a response to the symbolic violation of the part of himself that he secretly considered to be feminine – his sensitivity to offence, his love of music, and so on. He had unconsciously experienced the bronchoscopy as a homosexual rape.

Some patients who seem unable to use a visual art may be able to use a verbal art, such as poetry or storytelling. As we have seen, children often do this spontaneously, and it seems more effective if the words can be recorded on tape or written by the patient or therapist. The idea of writing about their work may appeal to adult patients who tend to limit their visual work to stereotyped images or patterns, caricatures, and so on: written words provide an opportunity to develop beyond a superficial meaning. A patient who is restless and easily distracted can sometimes be helped by the discipline of writing something, revising it, reading it to himself, or to the therapist, or having it read to him. The therapeutic benefit seems to lie in the self-confirmation that this work brings, rather than in producing 'eureka' insights. I think that the Incredible Hulk used my writing of the memory of the traumatic telephone call to confirm what he had realized already.

I have initiated some forms of writing in therapy with children that might appear drastic if taken out of the context of the ongoing work. For example, seven-year-old Julie had lived in residential care since she was three. She spent a lot of her time on someone's lap, wiping her runny nose on their overalls. She was not accepted as a playfellow by the other children and was considered dull and possibly brain-damaged. Julie was left-handed and was said to be unable to deal with writing, for she scribbled malformed letters from right to left. She dictated some stories to me about her drawings and clayworks, and I took them down, writing, like her, from right to left. She could not read back the story, and when I read the words to her in this order she reprimanded me ferociously, giving me several pages of homework. During the following sessions her need to create stories asserted itself and she wrote them for herself the right way round and asked me how to spell some of the words she needed.

By using her left-handedness in the way she did, Julie was able to fulfil her carers' expectations by low performance. When she needed words as a creative art she was able to dispense with this symptom. Another example of the therapeutic value of creative writing was shown by Miss Wright, a sensible old lady of 90, who caused grave concern in a residential home by her refusal to get out of bed. She had originally agreed to leave her own home for a rest, and when she found that she could not get back home again she lay down flat and pulled the sheet up to her chin. I was asked to call on her because she had been an art student in Paris in her youth. She was quite willing to talk about this but said that she no longer had any interest in drawing or painting. When we got acquainted she confided to me that, as she lay in bed, a few lines of verse would sometimes come to her, and I suggested that she wrote them down. In due course she produced long poems, written in couplets. Following this 'outburst', as she called it, Miss Wright got up and resumed her talent for drawing portraits from life. She has continued to live in the residential home and leads an active life, walking out, entertaining, and writing poems beyond her hundredth birthday.

CREATIVE WRITING AND THERAPEUTIC INTERVENTION

I aim to intervene in therapeutic sessions as little as possible, but there are occasions when I feel forced to enter the sacred play area and bring to light a communication that would have been better left to become explicit in the patient's own good time. When a child's overt symptoms have faded as a result of his creative work, his parents or carers reclaim him as an ordinary child and often take him out of therapy before he is ready to leave. An older child or adult may make the same decision about the part of himself that he feels to be dependent. The wound caused by an untimely break in therapy may be eased by a calculated intervention, even though it forces an issue and force begets counterforce. In any intervention I feel the need to protect the patient's identity when talking to him about himself, as I would if I were to talk about him to someone else. If the patient is a storyteller my interventions can be couched in his idiom and also take the form of a story.

Therapeutic work that is concerned with creative imagery can uncover a positive impulse behind ideas that might be otherwise dismissed as concrete, regressed thinking, or word salad. An apparent misuse of words is then found to be the patient's attempt to bring meaning to ideas that he finds vague, inaccurate or threatening. Creative initiative in the use of words can be sadly misunderstood if the creation is by someone who is known to be mentally ill. For example, an autistic three-year-old persisted in distressing play with units of a toy village, lifting them up and replacing them endlessly, crying 'houses' don't move, houses do move. Churches don't move, churches do move' until his parents were exhausted. This seemed insane until his mother discovered the symbolic imagery and realized that the boy had overheard her talking about the possibility of moving house.

For the final example of the Traditional Linear style and its association with visual and verbal thought, I return to the Incredible Hulk, the six-year-old boy I described in Chapter 5, to show the use of clay in his recovery from an amnesia. At the time that I started work with him his classwork was deteriorating, particularly his writing and spelling. His paintings gave some idea why this area of written, rather than spoken, words had been affected.

The Incredible Hulk appeared to have a good opinion of himself; he seemed to live as a body ego and enjoyed life at home and at school. He just did not seem to understand the suffering that he inflicted in his bouts of mindless violence, in which he would attack any living thing, man, boy or animal. As his condition became worse he could not be allowed to leave his house or garden without his mother or grandmother; but in spite of this his grandmother described him as a loving and lovable child.

The Incredible Hulk enjoyed painting. He worked at the easel, using the paint and brushes with flamboyant skill. At school he had learned to use the right amount of paint so his work rarely dripped, and he cleaned the brushes thoroughly each time he needed a change of colour. His first use of the paint was to make hand- and foot-prints that seemed to confirm his bodily presence for him, and then, using the Archaic Linear style, he copied the designs knitted on the front of his jumpers, obviously enjoying the opportunity it gave to stare down at his distended chest, like a miniature

Figure 10.2 *D-shaped house* Traditional Linear

Popeye. The Hulk also painted scenes from his everyday life, his school, his grandmother's house, and so on, showing himself in the middle of things, arms outflung and fingers or fists at the ready (Figure 10.2). At night a different picture emerged, for he suffered badly from nightmares and this led to a fear of the dark and for the safety of his guinea-pigs at night.

The Hulk worked with me for an hour each week, and in 20 sessions he made thirty-five paintings on large sheets of coloured card, 22 × 15 inches. He also made a few small drawings with coloured pencils during the time he was away with bronchitis. The first eleven paintings illustrate himself, his hands and feet, and the jumper designs. Day-to-day life at home and at school were first shown in plan (Figure 10.3), then he used the clay, and at this time began to organize his paintings along a base-line. In each of the last thirteen paintings the subject matter was placed between ground and skylines, an organization that persisted even when he painted a deeply disturbing experience (Figure 10.4). This change in style indicates a change of attitude from the sensuous dominance of the Archaic Linear style to some inclusion of ideas about external reality seen in the Linear Transition.

In this chapter I will draw attention to the features that show the Hulk's use of visual thinking. His progressive failure to write and spell seems to

Figure 10.3 *'The colours house'* Linear Transition

have been caused by a regression to visualizations and symbolic equivalence in these areas. For example, in his painting of his school, he showed the doorway as if filled with the letter M, which seems to be an equivalent image of his mother. Most conspicuous was his recurring use of a D shape. This occurred in seventeen paintings, as windows, doors, cars, school, and garden, as well as the shape of his own body. It was obvious that the D shape had become a substitute for the repressed memory of his daddy and as such would not be seen merely as a character to be used in spelling or writing. Moreover, his use of a D shape in depicting his own body suggested that he had incorporated his father and was living out an introjection during his outbursts of violence. Even when the Hulk had recovered from the amnesia, he continued to use some D shapes; for instance, in Figure 10.9 we can see two windows drawn in this way, with an A placed between them.

The Hulk also showed visual thinking in a heraldic use of colour. Warm colours – red, brown and pink – indicated himself and his mother, while babies were painted white. The unusual jade green that he first used to paint his hands was reserved for images that eventually became associated with his father. It first appeared as a line of scribble placed outside an enclosure (Figure 10.3) and also replacing his mother's ears (Figure 10.5).

Figure 10.4 *'The green person at night'* Linear Transition

This colour was also used in a painting of my house as the area of the roof space, in his last session before the Christmas break. During this period his mother reported that the Hulk had become rather ill with bronchitis for the first time in his life, and when he came to the session following the holiday he painted Figure 10.3, building up the shape with short strokes of different colours. His manner did not seem stressed or unhappy but I noticed that he worked very hard, cleaning his brush between each stroke. The jade green colour appears in one upper window and the frame is assembled in other

Figure 10.5 *Princess with green ears* Archaic Linear

colours also. The shape has been overpainted as a curve, like the lower part of a D shape. The opposite window was surrounded by two rows of dotted lines, that the Hulk called 'snow'. The overall effect of the facade is a worried and fragmented 'house-face'. The significance of the rows of dotted lines seem to indicate a failure to encircle or contain the self in the house square. It reminded me of the fragmented circles in Pippi's painting of '*The Big I*' (Figure 3.6). As usual, the Hulk's work pleased him and he called it '*The colours house*'. Some weeks later the Hulk's mother informed me that her husband was visiting them again and that the Hulk was tired and depressed after his illness. The Hulk had recognized his father and I had the whole story from his grandmother, who was not sure whether this had

Figure 10.6 '*A colours story*'   Archaic Linear overpainted Massive

happened before or after Christmas. The whole family were thrown into conflict by the unpredictability of these visits and she could see that the Hulk was overexcited by his father. Therapy had restored his memory but made him vulnerable to the family conflict. His mother considered that his depression was only the result of the bronchitis; she said it had knocked the stuffing out of him. She still saw him as a bad-tempered little boy but she thought that now he was no worse than other children. Once the Hulk had stopped his anti-social behaviour, his mother could not understand that he still needed help. In place of her earlier anxiety about him she now had the worry about the effect of her ex-husband's visits on both her children. She forgot that the Hulk had seemed dangerous and decided to buy paints for him and teach him herself, at home. The Hulk's state of mind at that time was indicated in a painting called '*The green person at night*', in which a figure approaches a house that seems almost to recoil. The house, ground, and sky are painted black, the windows blue, and the door green, like the figure. Two pink flowers are painted at either side of the house, and a red sun and black moon are in the sky (Figure 10.4).

Although the Hulk's social worker was concerned about him, his young mother was adamant that he no longer needed help. I felt that the best I could do was to take up her idea: to invite her to join the final sessions and see for herself the benefits of creating art. I also hoped that she might paint freely with him and share his play. After years of anxiety about her son this might be a special opportunity to enjoy his company. Anyway, it seemed the most that I would be allowed to do. The Hulk was delighted when this idea was put to him.

Contrary to my usual way of working, I took thought beforehand and prepared a short story that I could use if they were shy of starting to work. It did come in useful and both enjoyed listening. As soon as I began to read to them the Hulk flung himself in his mother's lap and sat with his arms round her neck. I called the story 'The princess and her son.'

> Once upon a time there was a beautiful princess with fair hair and blue eyes. She had one son whom she dearly loved and he had sparkling eyes and black hair. One day the princess called her son to her and said, 'My dear son, I have to go away to a far country and while I am gone I want to be quite easy in my mind about you. I want to know all that you want to tell me. But in our country there is no writing and no reading.' 'Never fear,' said the son to his mother, 'I will paint some lines and colours on paper and you will be able to see all that is in my heart.' Then the mother said, 'My dear son, that will do very well, and I will paint lines and colours for you, and in this way we shall keep in touch with each other although we may be far apart.'

Without hesitation the Hulk and his mother began to paint, one at each end of the room. They both used the Archaic Linear style. The Hulk made two pictures, one of the princess with arms outspread under a sunny sky (Figure 10.5) and the other of the son in which the centre of his painting was taken by the son's large outstretched hand. Meanwhile, his mother painted the princess standing outside her house in the sunshine and added a tiny figure in white at the top, on the right of the sun. She smiled at me as she said how much she had enjoyed painting in a way that he would understand.

The Hulk was deeply disappointed when she did not come again. He set up all the previous week's work along the wall and studied them. Finally, I asked him if there was anything more to be added to the story, and, instead of working on a new sheet of paper, he overpainted the big hand he had given the son in his painting, using many different colours including the jade green (Figure 10.6). Then he came to a stop and seemed nearly in tears. I asked again if there was more to the story and he immediately told me that there was 'a colours story'.

The boy went into the dark colours, away from the sky and the sun. He was all covered up in it and it was all dark colour like night-time. He went through the red and the green and the blue and yellow and then

Figure 10.7 *A man with a baby in his hand* Linear Transition

dark blue and then he saw a green person and he said 'Hallo' and the man said 'Goodbye'.

I said that I hoped that this was not to be the end of the story. I asked if he could paint what happened next. He directly chose some pink paper and drew on it a figure in brown paint, adding yellow hair and ears. Its outstretched hand seemed to reach towards a second figure that was painted in white (Figure 10.7). I asked if there was another story. At first the Hulk shook his head but then he asked if I would write it down. The Hulk dictated:

So the boy went into an orange place and there was a man with a present in his hand and he opened it up and he saw it was a little baby. It was a nice little baby and the man took the baby home.

After this the Hulk became very animated and offered to make a drawing to show how they went in by the back door (Figure 10.8). He drew this with coloured pencils and felt-tipped pens on ruled paper, below the story he had dictated, and then offered yet another story, to which he added a final drawing.

The house has one bedroom, a large bathroom and a toilet and a purple bedroom. Downstairs was a front door and a back door and at the back

Figure 10.8 '*The man took the baby home*' Traditional Linear

door was a person in red knocking for the baby to come out and play and the baby will come out to the person in blue and they *will* all play together.

He then made the final drawing, which showed the house with a narrow base (Figure 10.9). The upper floor has three windows: a square one on the left and two D-shaped ones with a letter A between them. The ground floor shows two doors and a single D-shaped window. The garden fence is shown as a base-line.

Although I could not work with the Hulk again, I heard from his social worker that no further trouble had been reported, although she found the Hulk a quiet child now, inclined to lie about. I saw him again after six months when he came to collect his paintings. He intended to put them up all round his bedroom and spent some time showing me each one. While looking at the painting of the prince, who became the boy in the colours story, I mentioned that it reminded me of the hand-prints he had made when he first came during the previous year. He replied, 'I was the Incredible Hulk, then Daddy was, and THAT'S THE END OF THE STORY.'

Figure 10.9 '*They will all play together*' Linear Transition

SUMMARY

Traditional Linear art is shaped by thoughts. It transmits ideas through formal representations or attributes of objects in a more or less schematic way. Some works are overloaded with detail and the artist has to include each blade of grass in a field and every brick of a house. Some Traditional Linear art is rather diagrammatic: it may be a caricature.

Emphasis upon thinking might be seen as a means of inhibiting feelings or limiting associations within rational bounds. This tends to impoverish the artist's creative initiative by rigid or obsessive habits of thought. In some cases a patient's only means of self-realization seems to be destructive. In some cases, verbal art, rather than a visual one, seems to be a more appropriate means of expression. By continuing with the case of the Incredible Hulk I have been able to show further the little boy's use of thinking and its effect upon his painting and stories, as well as the clay-work described in Chapter 5. Thought had been blocked in the area of an intolerable ambivalence towards his father yet this localized inhibition had not affected his basically thinking attitude to life. His style and attitude did not change very much throughout his work with me, remaining mainly in the area of the Linear Transition, quite closely associated with the Traditional Linear style of representation, seen in such pictures as Figure 10.8. The development of his plan-type drawings to square house facades may be symbolic of his growing need for an enclosing space when the memory of his father began to edge towards consciousness. He used some massive in-filling of small shapes, but heraldic colouring seems to have been the main means of moving between the Archaic styles. He only overpainted in full mass once, in the picture 'A colours story' (Figure 10.6), an impetuous illustration of the violence of his emotional conflict.

Figure 11.1 *Duck and frog* Linear Transition

Chapter 11

The Linear Transition
Dismantling and dismembering

This chapter will discuss the Linear Transition; this is the area in the circle of styles that links the Traditional Linear to the Archaic Linear and so completes the circle of styles. I shall also discuss the degree to which one of these two basic styles may predominate, and indicate the particular characteristics that arise when the unconscious attitudes they represent are equally powerful.

THE APPEARANCE

An artist working in the Linear Transition does not present the natural, three-dimensional appearance of his subject. The Linear emphasis imposes a formal, two-dimensionality upon its images; its subject is usually presented in small-scale detailed work in the style closest to the Traditional, and using larger, more open effects as the style approaches the Archaic. Colouring may be heraldic or local, and outlines inflexible or short and bold. The landscape (Figure 11.2) is an example with the Transitional area closest to the Traditional; the main part of the subject is treated conventionally, with local colouring and broken lines, while the Archaic element is suggested by some small symbolic drawings in the foreground. Picasso's cubist painting of a weeping woman is a superb example of the expressive force of integration of the two styles. The patient who knew of this painting decided to reproduce it from memory (Figure 11.3). The original maintains a balance between abstraction and representation, but the patient was more concerned with the subject matter and therefore emphasized the representational aspect. Works that fail to integrate the two styles may give an effect of meaningless disorganization in ways that seem perverse or bizarre: each style may even destroy the effectiveness of the other.

POSTURE AND GESTURE

Tension, excitement and restlessness often accompany this art style. Pippi's restlessness blocked his creative initiative altogether when he first

Figure 11.2 *Landscape* Linear Transition

Figure 11.3 Memory drawing of Picasso's '*Woman weeping*' Linear Transition

approached the art materials and Freddie released his tension by waving and swaying over the paint pots like a little dervish, dancing in ecstasy. Unlike the Traditional Linear artist, whose art work is usually painstaking and laborious, Linear Transitional art is made, expertly, as we saw in the paintings by the Incredible Hulk who even made hand-prints without getting paint on his cuffs. His sensuous expertness was particularly evident when he cleaned his brush before using a different colour. When he made '*The colours house*' (Figure 10.3) and used short strokes of different colours this finesse seemed to help him to control his anxiety.

The Linear Transition is often adopted by patients who have a physical disability, who come to therapy with an unrealistic expectation of achieving a facile skill in representation. At first they may be intimidated by the forcefulness of bright colours and the fluid suggestibility of paint and need time to find a way of working that will allow them to integrate the sensuous and conceptual needs.

REVERIE AND FANTASY

It is not easy to discern moments when reverie absorbs the patient and his fantasy leads him beyond his belief that art must first be completed in thought before it can be carried out. The art work may be sketchy, look unfinished or even deliberately fragmented. If the circle is found, it may only appear in part, suggesting that it is felt to be too big to be encompassed in a square (Figures 11.5 and 11.9).

When representations of whole objects have been chopped up into isolated bits they given an impression that the artist's unconscious fantasy is concerned with dismantling or dismembering.

Freud studied the symbolism of dreams and found indications of unconscious thinking in visual images that correspond to prehistoric language forms. These forms include displacements of emotion and condensation of several ideas into one. Such images show 'an inclination to form fresh unities out of elements which in our waking moments we should certainly keep separate' (Freud 1949: 29). Goya's aphorism, 'the sleep of reason begets monsters', underlines a general assumption that sensuous dominance destroys rational thought, causing its disruption, mutilation or dismemberment, according to the degree of conflict. The Linear Transitional style often reflects conflict between sensuous life and rational thinking, or offers a precarious union between them that nevertheless startles us with the violence of caricature. Cubist and surrealist art tilt our perspective of the everyday and chop up familiar configurations like works by a homicidal maniac. Contained within the aesthetic of integrated form they appear to be images of dissociated states or the extravagances of the split-off intellect. Some patients see in them their worst fears that madness would be uncovered by spontaneous art and they remain struggling with a technique for representation that is quite inadequate for their expressive needs. In fact, fragmentation and its distortive effects can occur in any style as an image of damage to the integrative power of the basic circle in the square; in this particular style the main disruption occurs in the area of thinking, when access to sensuous reality has been blocked. A dramatic example of the process of disintegration is given by a series of drawings of William Tell and his son (Schmidt *et al.* 1961: 50–1). The drawings show the figures progressively distorted by a stereotyped outline that is filled with a mosaic of lines until the child's body is indistinguishable from his father's leg. The third drawing shown indicates the anguish of this incorporation in the facial expressions that survive the process of fragmentation.

The artist Leger indicates the positive value of this style as a means of destroying configurative art:

> The life of fragments: a red fingernail, an eye, a mouth. The elastic effect produced by complementary colours which transform objects into some other reality. He [the artist] fills himself with all of this, drinks in the whole of this vital instantaneity which cuts through him in every direction.
>
> Abstract art is dominated by the same desire for complete and absolute freedom and perfection which inspires saints, heroes, and madmen. It is a peak on which only a few creative artists and their admirers can maintain themselves. In fact the very danger of this peak is the rarefied atmosphere by which it is surrounded. Modelling, contrasts and objects all disappear.   (Leger 1963: 200)

Leger's vision seems a cutting edge, separating self from other through the process of artistic creation. Freddie demonstrated the instantaneity of unmodified sensuous realization when he danced with delight before a sunlit tray of paints. However, when he started to use them he limited himself to a few cool colours (black, green, and blue), as if he realized, as Leger had, the precariousness of such sensuous heights that could result in finding images so empowered by the inner world that they could engulf a fragile ego.

THERAPY

The styles in which images are shaped contribute the essence of their meaning. Mixtures of Archaic and Traditional styles, seen in the area of the Linear Transition, reflect an integrating impulse to bring together sensuous and conceptual experiences to work in harmony. In art as therapy the success or failure of integration lies in the mind of the individual who creates the work: his images are not designed for other eyes. However, in so far as the therapist can follow the art work, he can be ready to facilitate the patient's search for symbols of integration if help is needed. The harmonious blend of Archaic and Traditional art is a way in which imagination can reach across the gulf that lies between adult and child art – the gulf in which so much creative integration can be lost. In her book *On Not Being Able To Paint* Milner (1986) attacks the rigidity of a Traditional art style in which she had been fixed from childhood. When her spontaneous doodles broke free they allowed her to express subjective feeling, to attack her objects in fantasy and release her creative initiative.

Poetic and metaphorical links between rational thought and abstract symbolism reflect the integrative function of the Linear Transition. Cadence, rhythm, alliteration and other non-rational qualities of poetry allow patients like Freddie to hear themselves speak about feelings that they cannot deal with in day-to-day life. If I put myself in the role of secretary, a patient can discover meaning as he chants or sings; the music of his words carries his thought along and he can, if he wishes, hear his stories and poems read back to him in my, different, voice.

As soon as Pippi created a story about his fragmented circles he could begin to take charge of the therapeutic hour. The conflict between his sensuous and conceptual experience had been given a visible form when the symbolic image of the fragmented circles enclosed the capital I. This allowed Pippi to see the need for something stronger than his inflated ego.

Adults may have greater difficulty in recognizing the need for change for they have invested in a powerfully intellectual attitude to life that has had considerable rewards. They need to give up the life of fragments, yet this may seem like a complete lack of control. Figures 11.2 to 11.6 indicate some of the ways in which I have seen the style appearing in works that have very different contents. All have treated the subject to a process of fragmentation, condensation and displacement, indicating that unconscious primary thinking has dominated rational thought. All were made by different people, but I have arranged them to give an idea of the degree to which each has been dominated by the Traditional or the Archaic aspect of the style. Figure 11.2 shows the patient's wish to transcend the limitations of traditional landscape painting by adding hieroglyphic symbols in the foreground. However, the small scale of these details does not indicate the power of transcendence that is obvious in works that are dominated by the Archaic Linear style; the little black images are more like cryptic memoranda. Figure 11.3 has been discussed already as a clear example of work that occupies the central area of the transition, and this is also true of Figure 11.1 which shows the ambiguousness of the message in an apparently innocuous painting of an underwater scene. Only on closer inspection do we see that its images have been dismembered in a way that both affirms and negates the sadistic illustration. We are shown the terror of the frog, yet, at the same time, the style denies any reality to its dismembered image. It is a visual denial of the feeling expressed. The sense of unreality also applies to the imagery portraying a football game (Figure 11.4) which is obviously dismembered and grotesque. The subject is barely maintained by the drawing of the football and the net; everything else is disjointed – a crude approximation of a face, a skirt, a terrace of houses, and so on. I find a vicious destructiveness portrayed in the style of these paintings which indicates the quality of the fantasies that have been expressed.

In the painting I describe as *Cat under table* (Figure 11.5), the disintegration has been modified by symmetrical organization. It suggests a sort of stability; the representational elements are still scattered, but the great shape of the half-circle, which has attributes of a table, provides an open area in which the patient has drawn a little cat. The style is still perched between Archaic and Traditional art, and the abstract patterns in the upper corners give a strange effect. The final painting in the series was entitled *Feet of clay* (Figure 11.6), and this style is closest to the Archaic Linear, but for the asymmetrical placement of the figure which is counterbalanced by the numerals. These, with the title, suggest an integrative impulse urging the patient towards a rational consideration of an otherwise frightening image of omnipotence.

Figure 11.4 *Footballer* Linear Transition

Figure 11.5 *Cat under table* Linear Transition

I turn now to the last four paintings shown (Figures 11.7 to 11.10), which give some idea of one individual's use of the style and its therapeutic change. The works were made over many months in an art group where each person's needs were met individually. The patient's psychotherapist had introduced him to the group and he attended punctually each week.

Figure 11.6 *Feet of clay* Linear Transition

Each painting shown represents a different phase of the patient's therapy, and in the changes of style we can see the way in which he recovered a sense of common humanity.

The patient, Heinz, was a clever young professional, a refugee from Nazi Germany. His appearance was immaculate and he used the English language with great precision. His manner was prefectly assured, but supercilious towards the rest of us, particularly those who were shabby, timid or less well-informed. Heinz had not trained as an artist but he quickly mastered the crude pastels that were provided, using the Traditional Linear style with wooden formality (Figure 11.7). He professed to be a great admirer of Hitler and carried a newspaper cutting of him reviewing the SS in his wallet. He copied this photograph several times, using it as a practice copy (Figure 11.8).

Figure 11.7 *Portrait from life* Traditional Linear

Repeated copying led to a degree of stylization, almost amounting to caricature, and when he became interested in this effect he turned to other power figures, such as Adler, Freud and Jung, showing them all with long red noses and thereby irritating their devotees in the art group. He explained to them the importance of disenchantment! His interest in the art of the malicious and bizarre led to images of little manikins, half goblin, half machine (Figure 11.9) – works that seemed to approach the Archaic in the symmetry and simplicity of the arrangements. After nearly a year of regular attendance, Heinz gave up pastel drawing and began to use paint; the strong outlines of his shapes were given up and the forms became Massive. Finally, his work showed strong emotional feeling in both style and subject, together with some naturalism in the effects of light an̄ space. Figure 11.10 reminds me of the Massive Transitional painting Rowanna made in which a volcano is set in a naturalistic background (Figure 5.4). Heinz placed his god of war on the left of the picture and filled the other half with a skyscape of bombing planes. The war-god was too big to be shown as a whole, while the bombers were given space. His style had moved half-way round the circle of styles, taking him from an excessively in-tellectual attitude – 'the rarefied atmosphere of absolute freedom and perfection which inspires saints, heroes and madmen' – to the human level

Figure 11.8 Copy of a photograph of Hitler Traditional Linear

of emotional commitment. Heinz's first style implied a state of mind in which emotion had no place, as he discovered when he tried to copy a picture of a girl in bathing costume but gave it up because the sensuous image could not be contained within the Traditional Linear style.

From this and other experiences of art work made in the Linear Transition, I can understand that it may become transfixed between the two modes. In such a case the style and content suggest that reality is experienced as a trap for the unwary. Fear of being duped provokes counter-attacks on emotional susceptibility, whether this is found inside or projected outward. A representational image is made that can be dismembered like an effigy of Guy Fawkes or Aunt Sally. The patient's denial of his destructive feelings forces him to lose touch with his positive feelings as well. Marion Milner brings this aspect vividly to life:

> how strong is the repression of love. We do continually crucify our imagination, kill our capacity for imaginative understanding of others, and for two reasons. It is partly because such understanding can bring pain and responsibility, but it is also due to our clinging to those principles of logical thought which require a duality, a split between subject and object, between seer and seen. Certainly we have to make that split

Figure 11.9 *Manikins* Linear Transition

Figure 11.10 *God of war* Massive Transition

if we are to emerge from the dependence of babyhood and manage the practical necessities of our lives, but where this principle fails is when it is given more than its rights in our relations with our fellow men.

(Milner 1987: 181)

SUMMARY

A transition between the Archaic and Traditional styles provides an area where their qualities can blend. However, if each style is equally potent the art work will be fragmented. The images reflect a disruption of continuity in the artist's sense of inner and outer reality which has been described by Leger as the life of fragments. If therapeutic space and time can be provided, the patient has an opportunity to create images that are wilfully dismembered. When these fantasies become visible in paintings or clay-works they can be worked through in feeling and thought. Changes in the style indicate the direction taken, either towards a more realistic under-standing of external reality or towards a stronger grasp of the subjective aspect of experience.

Chapter 12

Discussion

In this last chapter I would like to be able to present a neat gist of my study of the use of creative art as a form of psychotherapy. It is unlikely that I shall succeed because there is so much more to be learned and I seem to be only at the beginning: it may be too early to draw firm conclusions. For the past forty years I have tried to understand what is going on when we have the urge to create a work of art and, in particular, when stressed individuals seize on paint or clay and work avidly without guidance. A patient needs me to provide the space and time and to stay with him for this imaginative freedom to develop without interference from anyone, including myself and his own self-critical tendencies.

I know that creative work is essential in my own life. By creating art I affirm myself as a unique individual, capable of independent thought and action, and I must take the consequences – such as the pain of rejection if my creation is not accepted. The fear of failure is very strong: if my art is ignored, misunderstood or condemned, does this mean that I am bad? Will I be thought presumptuous, or accused of cheating? Dare I risk self-discovery? Will my work have any value outside my imagination? Some people cannot bear to find out if they have originality; they only re-create the work of others. When art is therapy, an individual has an opportunity to question his assumptions and work on them in his own way, as Rosie, Freddie, Teresa, Heinz and all the other people did.

When I hear people exclaiming that they wish they could paint or draw, and see how much they are attracted to the yielding qualities of paint or clay, I have a strong impression that we all need to create a symbolic image at certain times in our lives. The patient who is deeply absorbed in such work has moved beyond concern with the opinion of other people, he needs to communicate with himself. Winnicott says that it is creativity that makes life worth living, and when we cannot be as creative as we need to be in life, it is natural to turn to art, as children do.

Although I have a workable idea about the value of art as therapy, I have found this understanding extremely difficult to describe in writing. This is because the experiences that formed the theory in the first place were essentially non-verbal; they were the art works themselves, and I do not know how I can write about visual images without simplifying and even distorting them. Koestler is very clear about the limitations of written language. He says: 'words are a blessing that can turn into a curse. They crystallize thought, they give articulation and precision to vague images and hazy intuitions, but a crystal is no longer a fluid' (Koestler 1970: 173). My mental images and intuitions do not seem hazy or vague to me until I try to write them down; then, the ideas that are so economically stored in visual recollections have to be forced into logical patterns of thought. I have to describe mental processes that are simultaneous as if they occurred serially, as if they had distinct stages. Although I rarely recognize any boundary between reverie and fantasy I must make a verbal distinction between them. The creative image is timeless, as we see when an old person paints like a child and a child such as Nadia draws like an adult using the Traditional Massive style. Some senile patients can paint with this degree of naturalism, although they have never painted before and can no longer recognize those around them, from one day to the next. Moreover, it is a remarkable thing that we can respond to paintings made 20,000 years ago by people who may not have had any verbal language.

I was encouraged to know that Freud also found difficulty in describing the multiple processes of mental life and said:

> We have no way of conveying knowledge of a complicated set of simultaneous processes except by describing them successively, and thus it happens that all our accounts err in the first instance in the direction of oversimplication and must wait until they can be supplemented, reconstructed and so set right.   (Freud 1949: 77)

I do not know how I could have described my ideas about the significance of art styles without setting them in fragments of living history, yet such snippets, taken out of their own context and put into mine do not do justice to the continuous efforts and drive of the individuals' therapeutic work. These living experiences can easily read as fictions, and my choice, made with hindsight, of suitable examples might give the impression that I could foresee how an individual was to proceed. This is not so: I may understand what he *is* doing but I cannot know how things will turn out in the end.

I understand something of what goes on by artificially dividing style from content. This enables me to identify the unconscious attitude that is expressed in a particular style and follow its effect upon the patient. I find it is the style rather than the content of a work which stimulates a patient's need to extend beyond the boundaries of an habitual attitude. No style is itself pathological, but any style can reflect a rigid habitual attitude if it persists, totally unchanged, in a series of paintings or drawings, showing a stereotyped response that is inimical to living reality and the exigences of changing life. Some people bring their inappropriate lifestyle into their art work for long periods unchanged. They seem to need this time to hold on to worn-out attitudes before they can risk the effects of a spontaneous response to the art materials. Little Clarice showed early evidence of this anxiety in her repetitions of the stereotype she had learned (Figure 3.3).

John's paintings (Plates 7.1 to 7.6 and 8.1 to 8.6) are examples of a response to art materials that is uninhibited; a free uprush of creative energy that finds an outlet in paint and paper. I was able to record his ever-changing styles in the margin of my notes using a 'clockface' (Figure 1.1) with the hour hand indicating the present style. I can use this device when discussing patients' work with colleagues, and if therapy continues over many months or years the changes of style can be conveniently shown by setting them out in the form of a graph. In this way changes that are temporary moods can be distinguished from those which have a long or permanent effect.

As I sit waiting while patients paint I notice the recurrence of big, simple, symmetrically arranged shapes in many preliminary scribbles or doodles. These circles and squares, as I call them, might later become hidden under detail or ornament. They originate during a mood of abstraction or reverie rather than when the art work has been consciously planned and executed. When I found this basic arrangement of circle in square in the earliest closed shapes of young children's art, I came to identify it with the image of self-integration that lies within the unconscious mind. Although I cannot prove that circles and squares are more than accidental, their regular appearance is closely connected with the importance that patients give to their work and the satisfaction they find in it. The geometric arrangement of the motif seems to imply a need to order and arrange compartments that are separate and yet remain one.

In some cases the circle is displaced from the centre, fragmented or minute in relation to the square, but even a quarter- or half-circle seems to have unconscious significance, as in Rosie's coastline (Figure 4.3) or Heinz's cartoon (Figure 11.9). A half-circle seems to suggest that the whole self feels too unknown, or large, or inflated by ego to be contained in the square of the pictorial area. When a circle expresses the right 'fit' for a patient, however large or small it might be in proportion to the square, the patient shows a sense of being ardently alive and elated by his work. Some patients speak of the effect as having a sense of coming together, of being centred in themselves; some indicate a place in the chest or stomach where this feeling is to be found.

When a Traditional painting is transformed into an Archaic work and details are painted out, it seems that a patient needs to strip down his picture to reveal its essential meaning as an image of the self. In other cases the Circle might be imposed on a representational painting, as we saw in Miss Rink's *Seascape* (Plate 1.3). Once released from their habitual attitude, patients' styles tended to move clockwise round the circle of styles: an

Archaic artist would tend to use some aspect of the Traditional in some works and the Traditional artist's work would include something of the Archaic values. This seems to show an impulse to use the therapeutic opportunity to go back and realize a particular attitude of mind. This so-called regression in service of the ego, or stepping back in order to leap forward, may be a temporary mood that draws the patient to an experience that has been dissociated in some way and cut off from full realization of all its implications, as, for example, the Hulk's traumatic telephone call with his Daddy. However, this regression may also have a deeper cause in the need to realize a particular way of experiencing life that has never been conscious before, or only in a confusing and rudimentary way which Jung describes as 'undifferentiated' (Jung 1963). For example, the child who knew that houses don't move was thrown into panic when he heard his parents talk of moving house. This boy had little awareness of feelings, and therefore his sensuous experiences could not be modified by them or help him to grasp a metaphor intuitively. When at last he discovered that he was not the same as a doll, he was able to split self from other and acquire some emotional responsiveness to life.

Chris, Teresa, John, and many others showed me a general tendency for the styles to move clockwise during therapy and then to return to the habitual, or original style when therapy is ending. There may be different reasons for why this occurs. The original style may be a tempor-ary regression as a defence of the self at a time when a new frame is needed to replace that of the shared therapeutic work. This use of a style would be similar to the reassertion of the symbolic circle seen in Miss Rink's *Seascape* and Jennie's overpainting in '*Stay here*' (Figure 3.5). Resumption of a style that occurred in a patient's first painting might also be a positive assertion of a preferred way of looking at things. In other cases still it might suggest the influences of nature and/or nurture. As can be seen time and again, no style and its accompanying attitude is patho-logical unless its exclusiveness impoverishes the other aspects of reality.

Transitions from one style to another can indicate positive or negative attitudes towards the style that is becoming incorporated. This negative may appear in the subject as well as the style, as, for instance, in Rosie's painting (Figure 4.6) '*The Basse*' (presumably a misspelling of base, or basest). The expression of such primitive emotion breaking through the sensuous attitude, as in Evelyn's painting (Plate 1.2), seems to have occurred as Rosie filled in the linear shapes; afterwards she could move fully into the Archaic Massive style in her painting of the rose.

Both adults and children may make up stories and poems, write them down for themselves, or tell me to do this for them. I chose Freddie's literary art as an example of the interchangeability of the arts of painting, claywork and verbal creation. They all reflect the same need for an image of integrated inside/outside and self/other. The image may be a hero, an animal, a landscape or a machine. Freddie created a good old man, a rhino, a boat and a balloon.

As Eric Strauss had foretold when I visited him, early in the 1940s; my experience in personal analysis had given me many important insights, especially in providing a standard for comparison. This had been particularly helpful in understanding the nature of the projections that occur when art is used as a therapy. These I see as akin to those that are normally cast upon people, places and things that excite our primary needs. When a patient's creative activity seems boundless to him, he will be enlightened and strenghtened by his self discovery and will respond with love and gratitude to the facilitating environment. We saw this in Pippi when he dictated the story of the purple circle and found it to be his head, his brain and the beautiful world outside, and also when he managed to create something in a minimal way, making the clay prints and seeing in one of them a house that was 'superb ... a hut, nobody is in it, it's full of clay and paint and things to play with ...'. In Chapter 4 I described how Rosie first hated and then came to love the art group and myself.

Jung contends that the creation of symbolic images is a means of becoming independent of therapeutic help:

> when a patient has seen once or twice how he is freed from a wretched state of mind by working at a symbolical picture he will thenceforward turn to this means of release whenever things go badly with him. In this way something invaluable is won, namely a growth of independence, a step towards psychological maturity.   (Jung 1949: 80)

Rosie's altered feelings for us were only one aspect of the profound change in her unconscious attitude to the whole world that appeared in her change of art style.

Teresa's paintings (Figures 6.1, 6.5 and 6.6) are dramatic examples of the power of projection upon art. Time and again Teresa's random scribbles took on the attributes of human goodness and badness until she said, 'I can paint a face green if I like.' Then the masses of convex forms that expressed her feelings became her own doing and she could withdraw the projections. Teresa's paintings show her 'growth of independence' and also her steps 'towards psychological maturity'.

A patient who cannot find himself like this must project his cause for suffering. It is deflected outward upon the therapeutic situation, which seems unbearably tantalizing. He hates the studio, it seems dark or dirty. Like Pippi he may see spiders' webs in it; he takes a dislike to the art materials – they are too difficult, or not good enough; and, above all, he hates the therapist who seems to hold the secret of mental freedom. As Freud discovered, all this may be discretely hidden or turned inside out and the negative projection may be fuelled by interpretations that heighten the patient's resistance. If projections have been deflected from the art materials for any length of time, art as a therapy is in grave danger of becoming a psychotherapy. A transference neurosis can develop and must be resolved if creative art is to be resumed. But I am an art therapist and not a psychoanalyst: I have not the temperament, aptitude or training to control the situation. The patient has forgotten that he has come to use paint and clay; he sits talking and, worse still, inveigles me into talking; we are without the non-verbal communication of art and my power of rapport. If I have been so unprofessional to allow this situation to occur, I must wait for the moment when I feel I can interrupt it, and take the consequences.

Although the final aims of art therapy and verbal psychotherapy are the same, and there are times when they are indistinguishable, art therapy has the advantage of direct access to a patient's creative initiative in both the primary processes and secondary elaborations that form our mind. The style and content of creative art make these processes visible so that patient and therapist can actually see the attitude to life which is projected. Some ordinary people have an intuition of this power of creative art; they doodle or write poems for themselves alone. Martha and Mary used this form of self-therapy. Martha told me of the spontaneous recurrence of a dream image at intervals over many years after therapy which eventually resolved itself when things got bad enough to demand her attention. Mary described one evening of active imagination in pursuit of a recurring doodle of trees. But not everyone has access to potter's clay or poster paint; not everyone has the psychic energy and self-trust to follow a fantasy and take the time to give it shape. It is hard to say to oneself, 'This is the moment when I shall turn from the attractions and duties of the outer world and let an image appear.' Time is needed for the preoccupation, the withdrawal, the inner reality to be acknowledged and the hand to follow.

> a desultory formless functioning, or perhaps a rudimentary playing, as if in a neutral zone. It is only here, in this unintegrated state of the personality, that that which we describe as creative can appear. This if reflected back, but only if reflected back, becomes a part of the organized personality, and eventually this in summation makes the individual to be, to be found; and eventually enables himself or herself to postulate the existence of the self.
> (Winnicott 1971: 64)

My need to understand what was going on out there inside people that I call patients had to include a search for the therapist inside myself. I could not be satisfied unless the effects I saw outside, in the patient's work and their way of working, were validated inside myself, and my own projections upon life, my own ways of seeing could become visible through my own art work. Then, in as far as I can see myself, I can see the patient; in terms of the basic symbolic image, the circle creates the square and the square creates the circle. In terms of art as a therapy, Winnicott sums it up:

Psychotherapy is not making clever and apt interpretations: by and large it is a long-term giving the patient back what the patient brings. It is a complex derivative of the face that reflects what is there to be seen. I like to think of my work this way, and to think that if I do this well enough the patient will find his or her own self and will be able to exist and feel real.   (Winnicott 1971: 117)

Art as therapy is a mirror that the patient makes to find his own self reflected.

References

Adamson, E. (1984) *Art as Healing*, London: Coventure.

Adler, G. (1948) *Studies in Analytical Psychology*, London, Routledge.

Argan, G.C. (1968) 'The Italian Cinquecento and Idealism', in R. Huyghe (ed.) *Larousse Encyclopaedia of Renaissance and Baroque Art*, London: Hamlyn.

Betensky, M. (1973) *Self-discovery through Self-expression*, Springfield, Illinois: Thomas.

Blake, William (1939) *Poems and Prophecies*, ed. Max Plowman, London: Everyman.

Cellini, B. (1927) *Autobiography*, New York: The Modern Library.

Chesterton, G.K. (1902) *William Blake*, London: Duckworth.

Clarke, K. (1963) *Leonardo da Vinci*, London: Pelican.

Copland, A. (1952) *Music and Imagination*, London: Oxford University Press.

Fordham, M. (1969) *Children as Individuals*, London: Hodder and Stoughton.

—— (1973) *Analytical Psychology: A Modern Science*, London: Heinemann.

—— (1976) *The Self and Autism*, London: Heinemann.

Freeman, N.H. (1975) *Nature*, 254: 416–17.

Freud, S. (1921) *Delusion and Dream*, London: Allen & Unwin.

—— (1948) *An Autobiographical Study*, London: Hogarth Press.

—— (1949a) *An Outline of Psychoanalysis*, London: Hogarth Press.

—— (1949b) *The Ego and the Id*, London: Hogarth Press.

Froude, A. (1900) *Lives of the English Saints*, Introduction to St Neot, London: S.T. Freemantle.

Gombrich, E.H. (1990) *Art and Illusion*, London: Phaidon.

Gregory, R.L. (1966) *Eye and Brain*, World University Library.

Grosz, G. (1963) in E. Protter (ed.) *Painters on Painting*, New York: Universal Library.

Hamilton, R. and Simon, R. (1980) 'Art as a Healer', *Geriatric Medicine*.

James, P. (1966) *Henry Moore on Sculpture*, London: Methuen.

Jung, C.G. (1949) *Modern Man in Search of a Soul*, London: Routledge & Kegan Paul.

—— (1963) *Psychological Types*, London: Routledge & Kegan Paul.

Kellogg, R. (1970) *Analysing Children's Art*, Palo Alta, California: Mayfield Publishing Company.

Kellogg, R., Knoll, M. and Kugler, J. (1968) *Nature* 208: 1129–30.

Koestler, A. (1970) *The Act of Creation*, London: Pan Books.

Kris, E. (1973) *Psychoanalytic Explorations in Art*, New York: Schocken Books.

Lawrence, D.H. (1990) *Love Amongst the Haystacks*, London: Penguin.

Leger, F. (1963) in E. Protter (ed.) *Painters on Painting*, New York: Universal Library.

Lowenfeld, V. (1965) *The Nature of Creative Activity*, London: Routledge & Kegan Paul.

McCourt, D., McLaughlin, A. and Simon, R. (1984) 'The art of ageing', *Changes* 2, 3: 93–7.

Matthews, J. (1984) 'Children drawing: are young children really scribbling?', *Early Child Development and Care.*

Milner, M. (1986) *On Not Being Able To Paint*, London: Heinemann.

—— (1987) *The Suppressed Madness of Sane Men*, London: Tavistock.

Moore, H. (1966) *Henry Moore on Sculpture* in P. James. London: Methuen.

Morris, D. (1962) *The Biology of Art*, London: Methuen.

Naumberg, M. (1950) *Schizophrenic Art: Its Meaning in Psychotherapy*, New York: Grune, Stratton.

Picasso, P. (1960) Catalogue of Arts Council Exhibition, Plate 35a.

Prinzhorn, H. (1972) *Artistry of the Mentally Ill*, Springer Verlag.

Raine, K. (1970) *William Blake*, The World of Art Library, London: Thames and Hudson.

Schaverien, J. (1987) 'The scapegoat and the talisman: transference in art therapy', in *Images of Art Therapy: New Developments in Theory and Practice*, London: Tavistock.

Schmidt, G., Steck, H. and Bader, A. (1961) *If This Be Madness*, London: Thames & Hudson.

Segal, H. (1986) *The Work of Hanna Segal*, London: Free Association Books and Maresfield Library.

Selfe, L. (1977) *Nadia*, London: Academic Press.

Simon, R.M. (1970) 'The significance of pictorial styles in art therapy', *The American Journal of Art Therapy* 9: 159–75.

——. (1972) 'Pictorial styles of the habitually depressed', *International Journal of Social Psychiatry* 18, 2: 146–52.

—— (1975) 'Art – a strategic and empirical therapy?', *Confinia Psychiatrica* 18: 174–82.

—— (1976) 'Pictorial styles in the art of children', *British Journal of Aesthetics* 16: 272–8.

—— (1981) 'Bereavement art', *American Journal of Art Therapy* 20: 135–43.

—— (1982) 'Peter: a severely disabled patient's triumph through art', *American Journal of Art Therapy* 22: 13–15.

Winnicott, D.W. (1971) *Playing and Reality*, London: Tavistock.

—— (1978) *Through Paediatrics to Psychoanalysis*, London: Hogarth.

—— (1979) *The Maturational Process and the Facilitating Environment*, London: Hogarth Press.

—— (1986) *Home Is Where We Start From*, London: Penguin.

—— (1988) *Human Nature*, London: Free Association Books.

Index